MW01115060

One Foot Planted
in the Center,
the Other Dangling
off the Edge:
How Intentional Leadership
Can Transform Your Church

Gordon R. Dragt

Millennial Mind Publishing
An imprint of American Book Publishing
5442 So. 900 East, #146
Salt Lake City, UT 84117-7204
www.american-book.com
Printed in the United States of America on acid-free paper.
One Foot Planted in the Center, the Other Dangling off the Edge
Designed by Troy D. O'Brien, design@american-book.com

Publisher's Note: American Book Publishing relies on the author's integrity of research and attribution; each statement has not been investigated to determine if it has been accurately made. The author and publisher specifically disclaim any responsibility for any liability, loss, or risk, personal or otherwise, which is incurred as a consequence, directly or indirectly, of the use and application of any of the contents of this book. In such situations where medical, legal, or other professional services may apply, please seek the advice of such professionals directly.

ISBN-13: 978-1-58982-494-2
ISBN-10: 1-58982-494-6

Library of Congress Cataloging-in-Publication Data

Dragt, Gordon R., 1940-
One foot planted in the center, the other dangling off the edge : how intentional leadership can transform your church / Gordon R. Dragt ; foreword by Doug Adams.
p. cm.
Includes bibliographical references (p.   ).
ISBN-13: 978-1-58982-494-2
ISBN-10: 1-58982-494-6
1. Church renewal--New York (State)--New York--Case studies. 2. Christian leadership--New York (State)--New York--Case studies. 3. Pastoral theology--New York (State)--New York--Case studies. 4. Middle Collegiate Church (New York, N.Y.)--Case studies. 5. Dragt, Gordon R., 1940- I. Title.
BV600.3.D72 2009
285.7'7471--dc22

                    2008050312

Special Sales: These books are available at special discounts for bulk purchases. Special editions, including personalized covers, excerpts of existing books, and corporate imprints, can be created in large quantities for special needs. For more information e-mail info@american-book.com.

One Foot Planted in the Center, the Other Dangling off the Edge:

How Intentional Leadership Can Transform Your Church

Gordon R. Dragt

**Senior Minister Emeritus,
Middle Collegiate Church,
New York City**

Foreword by Doug Adams
Professor, Pacific School of Religion
and the Graduate Theological Union

Dedication

To a loving and supporting family through all the years, and still: Gayle, Duke, Cassandra, Ted, Zebulon, Mabel, and Hang.

Gordon Dragt's 16 Tips for Turning Your Church Around

It's a Calling, not a job.

Be intentional. The journey from here to there won't happen automatically or by faint-hearted efforts.

Be a leader. Leaders lead.

Make the vision big. Keep the journey simple.

Just say yes: miracles of growth, new ideas, and including a greater diversity of people may follow.

Keep opening more doors into the church from the community and into the community from the church.

Pay the rent. Having a positive attitude; being a cheerleader for the congregation; and building relationships, trust, and goodwill will make the difference.

Don't go it alone. It takes partnerships to sustain the journey.

Transform the worship service into a worship celebration.

Use the arts, because it's biblical and it works.

Be an Evangelist and don't be bashful about it.

Leaders need to grow spiritually, too. Sustaining regular self-examination and spiritual growth is essential.

God blessed life with diversity, multiculturalism, multiracialism, and multi-sexual orientations. Get used to it.

Travel light. Don't let a heavy theology, liturgy, and spirituality weigh you down.

Some of the best clues to transformational leadership are in the Bible. Jesus is a great example.

Be prepared for hard work, perseverance, and an adventurous journey. Transformational leadership is not for the faint-of-heart.

What Did the Media Say?

"Middle Collegiate Church is where old-time religion gets some new twists ... a diverse congregation ... untethered by tradition."
The New York Times, 1996

"Middle Collegiate Church is the best church to worship at when the others won't have you back. It is the Coney Island of the Lord!"
The Village Voice, 2002

"Amen to That! From jazz jams to free grub, this church offers more than sermons and song – Middle Collegiate Church – Eclectic celebrations at this East Village pillar offer everything from jazz to current events. Post-celebration activities include social brunches, art exhibits, children's art workshops, and a variety of adult education opportunities."
Time Out New York Magazine, 2002

"A very special annual Christmas party for persons with HIV/AIDS is held at the Middle Collegiate Church. For the

160 people in attendance, the party is the highlight of the Christmas season. 'They do this for us every year,' says one partygoer; 'it makes us feel good.'"
NY-1 TV, 2000

"At the Middle Collegiate Church everyone takes part in the annual Martin Luther King, Jr. celebration: singing, clapping, and praying."
WNBC TV, NY, 2002

Contents

Foreword

Using the arts, dance, music, photography, and theater, Rev. Gordon Dragt brought together at Middle Collegiate Church in New York City persons of all ages, races, sexual orientations, and classes.

Facing the challenge of a nearly dead church, Gordon developed a thriving congregation that is a model of what others may do. He had the pastoral and prophetic sense to discover the gifts of many people in the wider community and the priestly sense of how to involve those persons' gifts effectively into a worship celebration that inspires with a wide range of music, dance, drama, visual, and other arts. Through the gospel choir, the after school arts, the photo art gallery, the dance and drama groups in residence, and many other ways, Middle Church drew a remarkable number of persons from the New York area into ministry and became a major teaching church for students from seminaries across the country that were informed and inspired by the annual January Center for Arts, Religion, and Education (C.A.R.E.) "Arts Ministries in New York" course.

Gordon's achievement at Middle Collegiate Church and

our course there along with his coming to the GTU to teach courses in Berkeley about leadership have been a very important part of my own life ministry. I am proud to say that I advised Middle Church to hire Gordon in the first place many years ago. I then consulted with him and often visited Middle to aid him as that church grew from a dying congregation to a current ministry of over a thousand people each week.

I'm pleased that the relationship between Gordon, Middle Church, C.A.R.E., and me was important in transforming his church. I have done similar consulting with other churches, but Gordon's efforts at Middle Church excelled more than any other through the years. This book presents Gordon's proven strategy for turning around a church and I am honored to write the Foreword for it.

Dr. Doug Adams, Professor of Christianity and the Arts at the Pacific School of Religion, and chair of the Core Doctoral Faculty in Art and Religion, The Graduate Theological Union, Berkeley, California

Prologue

Walk through the celestial front doors of Middle Collegiate Church in the East Village and the first thing you notice are the dancers. Dancers? During a Sunday worship (celebration)? But there they are, in the green-carpeted space between the front pew and the altar, clad entirely in white, twisting sensually like refugees from a Twyla Tharp production. Minutes later, the gospel choir enters from a doorway to the side of the altar. A gospel choir? In a congregation descended from the Dutch Reformed Church? But there they are in a long line that proceeds up the right aisle, a heterogeneous parade of men and women: white, black, Hispanic, gay and straight. Presiding over it all is a beaming man in a brilliant red robe who seems as much a cocktail-party host as a conventional pastor. The Rev. Gordon R. Dragt seeks you out, pulling you into a handshake if he knows you slightly, a hug if he knows you well. As he chats you up, you half expect him to offer a glass of chardonnay, maybe even a canapé. What fun...

When this favorable review by *The New York Times* reporter Frank Bruni appeared in November 1996, those who recalled the chaotic state of Middle Collegiate Church in 1985 were amazed, bewildered, and shocked. Back then, at the most, fifteen-to-twenty-five worshippers sat in the pews. Sometimes there were more people in the choir than in the congregation, only one child in nursery, nobody cared too much about educational opportunities, and the outreach programs were limited to two tired efforts. Congregational decline and efforts to transform it were reoccurring themes in the past one hundred and fifty years of Middle's history.

In 1849, Talcot Chambers became the Senior Minister. Middle, once a thriving congregation, had declined to a small active membership with an even smaller worship attendance. Collegiate was contemplating closing the church and either renting or selling the building on Lafayette Avenue and 4th Street. Talcot's charge was to recreate the church and build a vital and growing congregation. Eventually it did happen, but not in the current location. A new Middle Church facility was built nearby on Second Avenue and 7th Street.

To its west was Astor Place, New York's thriving commercial district with large department stores and fashionable residences. To its east was the Lower East Side with its tenement housing and constantly changing and growing immigrant population. Located at the intersection of New York City's retail and immigrant population center, Middle again became a growing and blossoming congregation under Chambers' leadership.

When the city's commercial energy moved further uptown, many of the neighborhood's wealthy residents followed. The Lower East Side population expanded. The area changed. Middle became a causality that would plague the church for the next hundred years—aging leadership and a congregation unable to respond to the evolving social changes and cultural shifts taking place all around them. The city is a live organism constantly growing and changing. The church was slow to follow or to lead. Instead of viewing these changes as an opportunity to embrace, not a dreaded obstacle to fight, and an opening to adapt new possibilities for leadership and ministry, instead of a time of fear and loss, Middle entered into yet another phase of decline.

In 1932, Ernest Palen was installed as the Senior Minister in charge of Middle Collegiate Church. Prior to his installation, Middle had been a thriving congregation but had steadily declined in membership and worship attendance. Ernest's charge was to restart the church and build a revitalized congregation at the new location. He did just that, with a relevant ministry to the growing number of European immigrant families and a significant presence on the New York University campus. In the 1960s and 70s, however, the neighborhood dramatically changed. The families which had formed the foundation of the revitalized congregation moved out of the neighborhood to safer, less chaotic destinations, while other long-time members stayed and grew older. Ernest, too, became elderly and frail. Toward the end of a significant ministry, he was unable to appeal to the young arts persons moving into the neighborhood and was not prepared to cope with the monumental social and political change. Middle soon lost touch and relevancy. Turmoil not only surrounded the church, but also became the focus of the internal life and ministry of the congregation. Ernest was followed by several short-term ministries marked by either maintenance or turbulence.

In 1985, I became Middle's Senior Minister. Active participants had declined, the maintenance of the building had been deferred for years, the space was jealously occupied and controlled by a theater company, leadership was in chaos, there was no appropriate mission or vision for the struggling congregation, and the board had considered a motion to close the church. My charge was to create out of this chaotic internal and rapidly evolving external environment a fresh and growing congregation. It all sounded too familiar within the context of Middle Church history.

Ten years later, it was SRO with four hundred worshippers; not one, but three choirs; educational programs for parishioners of different races, creeds, genders, and sexual-orientations; outreach programs covering another thousand people; and a variety of children and youth programs.

How did this occur—how was life breathed into a church whose board had considered a motion to close it? And more important, how can what happened at Middle Collegiate Church help transform your congregation into a vibrant one that is alive with God's amazing grace?

In real estate, it's location, location, location. In resurrecting a stagnant, declining church, it's leadership, leadership, leadership. It is possible for clergy and lay leaders to become transformational leaders. Good transformational leadership and an ingestion of fresh and relevant ideas stimulated by the use of the arts can turn around a church. That is what this book is about.

Chapter One

Called
I guarantee it!

The journey I traveled with Middle Collegiate Church began in 1985, while living in Chapel Hill, North Carolina. I was the senior minister of a very active inter-denominational church. I loved living and working in "the southern part of heaven." My wife, Gayle, had a successful business and felt it would thrive even more in the clothing and fashion conscious environment of the northeast. Our son Duke was a senior in high school, looking toward college. Our daughter Cassie was a high school sophomore, enjoying friends and school.

On a trip to New York City, I had a conversation with several members of a Collegiate Church committee searching for a minister for Middle Collegiate Church located in the East Village on the Lower East Side of Manhattan. We left that informal meeting agreeing to continue our conversation. I had always felt if I was ever invited to serve a church in New York City, it was my obligation or calling to go, no matter where or what my current ministry was. Many people who contributed to the development and growth of our nation came through New York City. The city is also a welcoming home for people who would find acceptance and support difficult in other towns and cities in our country. Our nation is indebted to New York City. I believe we have a collective responsibility for the well-being of the city of New York's life and people, including its service institutions and churches. New York City churches should never be considered the last choice of clergy who would rather be in the suburbs or elsewhere, but the first choice of clergy who want to make a difference in a city that has made a big difference in the life of our entire nation.

In 1985, the East Village in New York City was rapidly changing from a stable immigrant family community into a raw and edgy arts environment. Middle Church did not make the transition. A senior minister who had a very successful ministry retired after forty years. His declining health toward the end of his long ministry corresponded with a declining church membership and worship attendance. The church was then served by a series of short-term ministers, some of whom had lost touch with the neighborhood and one who had a promising yet troubled tenure. Arts, restaurants, abandoned buildings, homelessness, drug dealers, creative vitality, bohemian energy, and entrepreneurial possibilities all described the neighborhood. Middle's worship declined to mostly elderly women, a few men, and a couple of younger adults, along with a handful of persons from the arts community whose participation seemed focused mostly upon protecting their free use of East Village space. I felt called to transform Middle Church into a thriving congregation with a new vision and ministry.

On one of many visits to Manhattan, I met Middle's interim minister who gave me a tour of the facility. Plaster was peeling, paint was fading, woodwork and carpeting looked dirty, the rooms were dark, the heavy wood doors were like fortresses to the outside, and people from a theater were rehearsing in most of the available space in the church house. The tour left the impression that Middle was an active theater space with a dying, unmaintained church attached. The good news was there was no place to go but up. And no way would I have ever considered coming to a thriving, vibrant city like New York to preside over the death of a church. I felt called.

I was invited back to attend a meeting of the search committee which would select two candidates. During the week leading up to the meeting, I was hospitalized in Chapel Hill and released with just enough time to catch a plane to the city. On the way to the airport, Gayle drove while I lounged with the front seat positioned as far back as it would go, too weak to sit up or to focus my eyes and mind. "Should we turn around and go home?" Gayle asked. "We don't have to continue the interviews at this time. There will be other opportunities."

"I'm at a critical point in the process," I replied. "We both like the possibility of living and working in New York City, and I want to see the search through to whatever end." We continued to the airport. No matter what condition I was in physically and emotionally, spiritually I felt called.

When we arrived at the hotel in late afternoon, I immediately went to bed. The meeting of the search committee was scheduled for early evening. The only thing I remember of the meeting was that one person said, "You have never lived in New York City. You have never worked in New York City. You have never had a ministry in any place like the current environment and condition of Middle Church and the East

Village. What makes you think you can come here and trans-form Middle into a vibrant and growing congregation?" Good question. I will never forget my reply: "I guarantee it. If I can't begin turning Middle around in three-to-five years to the point where you can see positive results, I will walk away from it, you will have no obligation to me, and I will thank you for giving me the opportunity to have tried." My response was not meant to be arrogant or thoughtless. It is what I felt and believed.

I was confident of my call to Middle Collegiate Church and what that call meant. I was confident of being surrounded by the Holy Spirit in my ministry. There was no doubt God trusted me to fulfill the call. God did not just pick me out of nowhere; there was plenty of preparation. Earlier in my ministry, I had experienced going to a church to which I was not really called. I knew what that was like. This was different. I guaranteed it, even if that was not generally acceptable church language.

I had already been in the ministry for twenty years, and it was not the first time I defied conventional practice. I started a church and reinvented churches in a suburb, a small town, and a university town. To me, there was no reason why the very same principles of church transformation, leadership, and growth could not be adapted to work in a city environment. Transformational, adaptive leadership was my calling. It was what I did best. So I had no difficulty looking the member of the search committee in the eye and saying, "I guarantee it."

Of course, when I walked out of the room, I wondered if the search committee was saying, "This guy is a fool. We are ready to close the church, we have had enough of Middle's dysfunctional life, and we are finished pouring money into that place without getting any positive results. He doesn't know what he is talking about. Nobody can guarantee they are going to transform a church like Middle with so many internal and external problems. I think we should cut him from consideration now, before we make another mistake and get one more person in there who will embarrass himself and us. Who is he to guarantee ministry, anyway?"

I was about ready to hail a cab, but instead decided to walk to the hotel. On the way, I gazed at all the lights. I was mesmerized by the many sights and sounds of nighttime in this great city. I watched many different people come and go in a continuous procession. My mind began to wander and to wonder. The walk seemed much longer than only a few blocks. Questions came and then quickly left without any of them ever requiring answers.

For just a fleeting moment, I was reminded of the story of Elijah, who was on the run from Jezebel, and finally made it to Mount Horeb. There he took refuge in a cave. Hiding in some remote area deep inside the cave, he desperately listened for a message from God. Elijah heard the powerful sounds of earthquakes, wind and fire, but God's voice wasn't in any of those sounds. He then moved his person and his life near the opening of the cave where he was at the same time both a little safe and a little vulnerable. There at the opening of the cave, Elijah heard a still small voice, asking, "Elijah, what are you doing here? What do you plan to do with your life here, Elijah?"

As I walked closer to the hotel, that is the question that wouldn't leave me and made my short walk such a long journey, "Gordon, what are you doing here in New York City, such a long way from where your journey began? What are you planning to do with your life here, Gordon?" Every time

I asked myself those questions, I kept hearing a call reaffirmed, dreams rekindled, creativity recharged, and imagining the future refreshed. I felt called. I guarantee it.

In the hotel room, we packed to go back to North Carolina. The next day began with a surprise telephone conversation inviting me to a final interview, during which the committee planned to select the person to receive the "grand prize" of living in the rapidly changing East Village and transforming a dying, dysfunctional church with a handful of active participants. I was confident, but nervous about the final step. The plan called for an early meeting the following morning during which we would be interviewed by a psychologist. There would be two witnesses from the search committee. More than a little apprehensive, there I was, sitting on a couch with the other finalist, the psychologist sitting in front of us, and the two members of the search committee on either side of the psychologist. It felt strange, but it got much stranger. The psychologist began pressing me hard, even pushing me into a corner about my inexperience in the city and my relevant skills to handle the chaotic environment of Middle Church and the East Village. The other candidate thought this was a perfect opening for him to jump in and help push me over the edge. My competitive nature kicked in. I thought to myself, this guy sitting next to me is a lightweight. I have way more experience than he does and why am I letting this psychologist abuse me? I turned to the other candidate, who had never held a senior minister position, and quickly ended his inexperienced chatter by describing a more patient, realistic, and inclusive vision of transforming Middle Church gleaned from twenty years of successful ministry in a variety of church and geographical settings. Then I responded to the psychologist's questions about my lack of familiarity with New York City and how I felt the principles of trans-formation that were successful elsewhere could be adapted to the city. The room was filled with silence and blank facial ex-pressions. The psychologist first looked at his notes, then at us. I blew it. I was relieved. The session ended and I quickly left for the hotel. Without much conversation, Gayle and I took a taxi to the airport, boarded a plane, and flew back to North Carolina.

Later that week, the chair of the search committee left a message on the answering machine. I figured it was just a courtesy call to tell me the obvious. It was a puzzling surprise when I heard his voice say, if I was still interested, the com-mittee wanted me to come to New York City. I felt called. I guarantee it.

Now the hard part. There is a human responsibility con-nected to every call from God. God did God's part. Now, to keep God's confidence and blessing, I would have to do my part to fulfill the guarantee. A dizzying and hesitant few weeks followed, trying to carefully finish a ministry in Chapel Hill, which I loved, and prepare for a very different ministry in New York City, which I anxiously anticipated. My mind overflowed and restful sleep was rare.

Do you ever have a word or a phrase or a song that just gets stuck in your mind? It keeps popping up at unexpected times all day long, and then reappears at night when you are trying to sleep. For me it's more often a hymn or a prayer, but during this time of transition it was just three words from the Christmas story. They remained unspoken and unex-pressed, yet always present, always challenging, comforting, and questioning.

The three words form a curious phrase that appears at the very heart of Luke's Christmas story: "In that region of the

11

Middle East, there were shepherds out in the field keeping watch over their flock by night. An angel of God appeared to them and the glory of God shone around them ... and the shepherds were filled with fear. But God's messenger said to them, 'Don't be afraid.'" Don't be afraid.

After all the miles, meetings, talk, and promises, and with three words swirling around in my head, I was beginning what more and more seemed like an impossible task. But I had faith that the very same angel, messenger, spirit, or presence of God who appeared to the shepherds in the Christmas story was in some amazing way appearing to me and to Middle Church during this important moment for both of us, with the very same startling, surprising message: "Don't be afraid." Despite all other mental messages competing for equal time, the message of the Christmas angel kept repeating: "Don't be afraid."

So there I was, and there was Middle Church. Both of us were standing at the very threshold of a new beginning—excited, anticipating, and yes, a little afraid. It was still the same old church, but we were not going to simply repeat the same old ways of being and doing or drag the old with us into the new beginning. Yes, a little afraid, but all the while hearing the voice of the Christmas angel graciously appearing, whispering, prodding, comforting, and challenging silently inside my own soul and the soul of this old church about to experience an Easter resurrection: "Don't be afraid." Don't be afraid of the past. Don't be afraid of the present. Don't be afraid of moving on into an unknown future. "Don't be afraid," says the angel to the shepherds and to me and to us. I still felt called. I still guarantee it.

One of the first things I did was to read the minutes of the board from 1890-1984. I learned that Middle had a history of thriving and creative ministries followed by times of decline and turbulence. A chart of Middle's history looked like a stock analysis with lines soaring upward followed by repetitive lines plunging downward. My charge was similar to that of Ernest Palen before me and of Talbot Chambers before him: resurrect a dying congregation into a vibrant, growing, and missional church. Reading these minutes gave me an opportunity to recognize and avoid a major negative pattern in Middle's past. From the very beginning, my intention was that Middle's yo-yo pattern of history was not going to repeat itself on my watch. For the past one hundred and fifteen years, new life at Middle was always temporary; it was seldom systemic. Twice the board discussed closing the church. Stagnation, decline, and near death were constant possibilities. That is the way it sometimes is with efforts to resurrect a church. If new life, ministry, and vision do not become part of the very nature and spirit of the church, resurrection efforts will only be temporary look-good experiences. It is easy to make a few quick fixes that give the appearance of turning a church around, but it is difficult and demanding work to systemically change a vision and direction of an ailing church for the long term. I wanted to be sensitive to the past, learn from it, and celebrate the good ministries of those who preceded me. I did not want to replay the destructive pattern that kept repeating itself. I was excited about discovering a new vision and focusing upon a new hoped for reality. I was determined to make good on my guarantee to resurrect in this place at this time a creative, relevant, diverse, and growing ministry that would not be followed by yet another period of chaos and decline. I did not come to the East Village of New York City to preside over the death of a congregation, nor did I come to lead a successful but only temporary ministry.

My charge was not to forget about the troubled past, rewrite Middle's history, or act like it did not exist, but not to dwell upon it, either; or worse yet, to focus upon it. I came to Middle Collegiate Church to intentionally "create a new thing in the earth," which would continue long after my time.

Several months into my ministry at Middle, the psychologist called to ask if he could come by for a few minutes to welcome me. I delighted at the opportunity because I had been waiting to ask him what in the world was going on in his office when the two candidates met with him during the search process. I told him there was one point in our conversation when I simply said to myself, enough is enough. I've had it. I'm not going to let you people walk all over me like that, so I took on the other guy who I thought was a weak candidate anyway. The psychologist said, "I know exactly the point in our conversation you are talking about. It was at that very moment I noted you were the person for Middle. The Collegiate Church needed a survivor, and I saw you as a survivor. You will still be here ten, fifteen, twenty years from now. I didn't think the other person would."

How do you like that? Of all the qualifications I felt I had for the ministry, I was selected for this position in New York City because I am a survivor. That is one quality of ministry they never taught in seminary. Survival is really about transformational, adaptive leadership, which I initially learned from my parents. It is also a bit of emotional learning that surfaced naturally throughout my entire ministry.

I grew up in a much loved, sheltered, and traditionally rich religious environment of a small Midwestern farming community. Within this protected setting I was graced with parents who were not afraid to raise me to appreciate the broad strokes of the Bible and tradition and to experience and respect a much wider diversity of people and lifestyles beyond those of my childhood surroundings. From my parents I grew up knowing what it means to live life with one foot planted solidly in the center while dangling the other over the edge. Within a conservative environment, on the one hand they were "insider people" with traditional religious values and regular church attendance, and on the other hand they were "outsider people" living progressive, entrepreneurial, on-the-edge lives.

In a diverse New Jersey town, I learned passion, compassion, and how to function in a team ministry. In a small suburban Pennsylvania community where a "new" church was started, the goals of creating a diverse, festive, and arts-friendly multicultural, multiracial, multi-sexual orientation congregation were addressed. In a small town in the Hudson Valley in upstate New York, difficult lessons were learned about the potential struggles and hazards of revitalizing an old, declining church. In a major university town in North Carolina, there were exciting experiences of how to minister and adapt in an unfamiliar cultural surrounding. There I discovered the fundamental principles involved in re-energizing an already solid justice, welcoming, and arts-friendly congregation.

I was surprised when I was invited to become the minister of Middle Collegiate Church in New York City. But I am convinced, the main task of the committee searching for someone to lead Middle's transformation from near death to a living, loving, growing, relevant, and unconventional ministry was to discover the one God had already called to bring this dying church back to life in this great and important city. I believe all the previous churches in which I served were in a very real sense preparation for the really big ministry to bring a dead church back to life in the heart of New York City.

How did I get here from there? I love that question. It sometimes haunts me. It is the Sarah and Abraham faith question. Some things happened along my life and faith journey that pointed me in the direction, long before I arrived at Middle Collegiate Church. Each stop along the way was significant, made an impact, taught me important lessons, and each ministry had integrity in-and-of itself. I was constantly restless, always wanting to push the boundaries of what a church can be. Like Sarah and Abraham, I traveled an ever-expanding journey of faith and trust, never knowing where the journey was leading. Every place I stopped, there was an important learning, a critical experience, sometimes a key personal or professional mistake made, and a new understanding of the responsibility and role of being a transformational leader. I believe I was called long before the search committee ever knew who I was and before I had ever heard of Middle. I am convinced I was nurtured and prepared for that moment all along the way. God called me to Middle Collegiate Church. The search committee's task was to select the person God had already called. My task was to understand Middle's long road to decline and make an equally long and intentional commitment to turn it around.

Chapter Two

Transformational Leadership Is Intentional
Ministry is not for the faint of heart

In most cases, churches don't become static, decline, or die overnight. It is usually a long process and sometimes goes unnoticed for years, just as it may take a long time for new life to be incorporated into a church's systemic ministry and identity. A transformational leader needs to understand that the commitment to turn a church around is not a short-term commitment. It took seven years at Middle before any of the seeds began to show signs of budding. And what a relief and how exciting it was when these first new buds appeared, even though there was still a lot of work ahead of us. Transformational, adaptive leadership is intentional. Intentional is a key word in every transformational leader's vocabulary. If decisions for new life are not intentional and purposeful, a church will simply continue to be stuck or dysfunctional or decline.

Not all church leaders can bring a declining or dying church back to life. Not even some of the most talented, creative, and gifted clergy can lead such a transformation. For many, the commitment is too large, the work is too demanding, the unanticipated personal toll is too great, and the transformational journey takes too long. To bring a dead church back to life requires a leader to singularly focus upon this unique and incredible, but personally challenging and demanding opportunity. To be an entrepreneurial, visionary, creative, or talented leader is not enough. To be a transformational leader requires a level of work, adventure, and dedication that is not often learned or experienced growing up in our society today. Ronald Heifetz warns that efforts for change and transformation "are not for the faint-hearted and are not faint-hearted efforts."[1] Faint-hearted efforts will simply create more of the same faint-hearted results. When clergy or lay leaders are asked what they would like most to happen in their churches, they often say they would like their congregations to be more diverse. Then they immediately follow with a list of reasons why they aren't or can't or won't be. Usually, it's the fault of the congregation or the neighborhood or a whole host of other uncontrollable circumstances. I believe it is more often a leadership deficiency. "We cannot become what we need to be by remaining what we are."[2] Lovett Weems says the usual first response when things aren't going well in a congregation is to do more of the same, more vigorously, which will just get us more of the same, more vigorously.[3] Diversity is intentional. Church growth is intentional. Welcoming is intentional. Multiracial and multicultural are intentional. Transformational, adap-

---

[1] Ronald A. Heifetz, *Leadership Without Easy Answers,* (The Belknap Press of Harvard University Press, Cambridge, MA, 1994), p. 239.

[2] Lovett H. Weems, *Take the Next Step: Leading Lasting Change in the Church*, (Abingdon Press, Nashville, 2003), p. 16.

[3] Ibid., p. 18.

tive, intentional leadership is the key.[4] Without it, don't even think about a vision of getting anything but more of the same. Churches don't start changing just because a person or an official board thinks it is a good idea to change. It won't happen.

Middle Collegiate Church became a growing, diverse congregation. A multicultural gospel choir was created by a member and deacon of the church who was a professional actor, singer, and dancer. Up-front worship leadership was intentionally diverse. Careful attention was given to who was invited to be preachers, associates, musicians, singers, worship leaders, greeters, performers, child caregivers, and church school and youth group leaders, so people attending Middle on Sundays would always see a church that placed a priority upon diverse up-front leadership. People of color, men and women, and lesbians and gays were invited by the board to become decision-makers and serve as elders and deacons on the official board of the church. Senior and associate clergy were intentionally selected by the Senior Minister and the board to fit a model of diverse leadership. Outreach into the neighborhood, the city, and the metropolitan region was intentionally multicultural, multiracial, and multi-sexual orientation. Advertising and the creation of special event concerts, conferences, educational classes, and speakers were purposefully and intentionally targeted to a diverse audience. The whole face, worship, and ministry of the congregation changed. Middle Church became systemically diverse. The same intentional leadership was exercised to include the arts in the worship and life of the congregation. Dance, theater, a variety of music and musical instruments, photography, and puppets intentionally appeared regularly

---

[4] Heifetz, *Leadership Without Easy Answers,* p. 22.

19

in Middle's life and worship. If it is not intentional, new life and diversity in the local congregation will not happen and certainly they won't happen for the long term, which is the ultimate goal. Systemic change is much different than making changes to simply look good. Transformational change is systemic when it becomes a part of the very nature of the church's life, ministry, and outreach.

A person from a church I once served said, "Gordon, the thing I like most about you is that you are always in the middle of things and that, after all, is what life is all about." I graciously thanked the person for what I am sure was meant to be a compliment, but quite frankly, I don't believe that about me and I certainly don't believe that about life. Church leaders can become so busy by being in the middle of too many on-going, expected, routine, maintenance, faint-hearted things that we don't even notice what is happening to the real dynamics or energy of the church.

At the beginning of the transformational process at Middle, I was also intentional about not being middle-of-the-road. A church will never bridge the gap between reality and a new vision by being middle-of-the-road or by performing a middle-of-the-road ministry or by doing more of what it has always been doing or by planning a series of faint-hearted efforts. The journey from here to there is not for the faint of heart. A congregation's transformational journey involves a continuous process of starting and stopping, discovering a vision and adapting to yet a new vision, always new beginnings and new endings, a constant movement back and forth from reflection to action. This process happens "over and over through the day, week, month, and year. You take action, step back and assess the results of the action, reassess the plan, then go to the dance floor and make the next move."[5] Discovering a transformational vision is where this exciting and challenging journey begins.

---

[5] Ronald A. Heifetz and Marty Linksky, *Leadership on the Line: Staying Alive Through the Dangers of Leading,* (Harvard Business School Press, Boston, MA), p. 73.

Chapter Three

Discovering the Vision
Aha! So...That's It!

In 1985 attendance at the first two worship celebrations was twenty-seven! On my second Sunday there, a bit discouraged already, I waited for everyone to leave, then sat behind Middle's old stone padded pulpit shedding a few tears of self-pity, praying to God, desperately questioning God, questioning myself, and questioning whether I actually had the right skills, energy, and faith to pull off the miracle that needed to happen on Second Avenue and 7th Street. I even questioned my call to the ministry and especially the call and confidence I felt about coming to Middle. Maybe I made a mistake. Maybe I didn't have the leadership skills to do it after all. Maybe I should not have been so positive to the search committee about my ability to resurrect this old church. Maybe I was foolish to "guarantee it." Later, I picked myself up, left the building, walked across Second Avenue to Moshe's Bakery, purchased the sweetest most sugary pastry I could find, walked out of the bakery, and stood in front of the shop indulging my self-pity and my questions in powered sugar. I must have looked like a mess standing there in a dark suit with white powdered sugar spilling all over the front of me. I stared across the avenue at Middle Church, focusing upon the many large rectangular limestone rocks stacked one upon the other. All of a sudden, what I later interpreted to be the Spirit of God—but others have suggested it could have been the sugar—spoke to me. The limestone rocks were no longer rocks. They became doors. Real doors. The kind of doors real people walk in and out of. The whole front of the church became hundreds of doors. Each door was unlocked and left slightly open. On each door was a sign that said "welcome" and another sign on which appeared a person's name or the name of a talent or race or culture or sexual orientation, age, human condition, gender, and so-on. All the beautiful diverse peoples, ages, talents, arts, and conditions of God's beloved creation appeared on those welcome doors. And I saw a whole mosaic of God's people walk by Middle Church, stop, glance at the building and, with surprise in their voice, say, "Look, that's my name on the door, and it says 'welcome.'" They opened the door and walked in.

"AHA! So ... That's it!" There were too few open doors leading into the church. That was our problem. We needed more entry points. We needed more open doors. We were too narrow here. We were not broad, diverse, inclusive, and welcoming enough. God was saying, "Gordon, your mission here is to keep opening more doors and welcoming more people, no matter who, no matter what, no questions asked. No matter where one is in one's life or faith journey, your ministry is to simply open doors and welcome people." That sounded a lot like being a schmoozer. Imagine such a calling for a leader in the church. I never heard anything like that when I was in seminary. Being a doorman and a schmoozer were never mentioned in the classroom or imagined for a seminary graduate. But that was my calling and my vocation for the past forty years. It was out of that vision that the miracle of Middle Church happened.

One of the important things learned from this "aha moment" is that vision is where transformation begins, and vision is more often discovered out of the experiences of ordinary life around us than created from complicated theories and procedures. Clues for transforming a church are all around us all the time, and as the environment and circumstances of a congregation constantly change, new clues are continuously evolving. One of the key responsibilities of a transformational, adaptive leader is to be alert to these clues and to bring them into the discovery process of an ever-evolving new vision for the congregation's life, worship, and ministry. For me, it was being spiritually overwhelmed by seeing the façade of the church building and passersby in a completely different, transforming way. I had looked at the church building many times before, but never like that. This time, it was "screaming" clues to a new vision for Middle to open more doors and create more entry points into the church and into the community from the church. This new vision demanded a new kind of leadership. "Leadership begins with vision. Leadership is about change. We cannot become what we need to be by remaining what we are. There can be no real leadership without significant change."[6]

I have sometimes humorously referred to my leadership style as ministry-lite, theology-lite, liturgy-lite, and belief-lite. The vision is big, but to carry out the vision is simple or

---

[6] Weems, *Church Leadership,* p. 37.

lite—to be a doorman, a producer, a schmoozer for God. That was my calling and I accepted the calling to keep opening more doors, creating more entry points, producing more worship parties, and welcoming more people—no questions asked, no requirements needed, no invitations necessary. That was the summary of my whole transformational leadership style. The vision was always expansive; the plan to bridge the gap between current reality and vision was always very intentional and uncomplicated. Vision is at the heart and soul of transformational leadership. It is where transformation begins. With vision, says the author of Proverbs, the people have life, hope, and a future. Without vision, stagnation and decline continue.

There is a fascinating story in Mark's Gospel about Jesus healing a paralytic who was lowered from the roof into the house where Jesus was. The house Mark is talking about is probably a small, one-story "row house" with a flat roof. The house is being used on this occasion for "church." Jesus is giving the sermon. The church is packed by all the regular folks—they are all there, but there are some folks outside who can't find a way to get into church. The focus of the story is on a particular person who, we are told, is paralyzed; he is different from the regular folks on the inside; he is left outside the church; he can't find an entry into church.

The paralyzed person has four friends who search for and find another way into church. They create another entry point. The house probably had steps leading to the roof. The friends carry him to the roof and start pulling it apart. While Jesus is preaching to all the regulars packed into the "church," debris from the roof begins to fall down upon their heads. At first it is just dust, but soon large chunks of material fall into the room below. Then a hole appears. The people look up and see a face looking down at them. The hole gets larger, and the people in church begin to move away so they won't get hurt and dirty from the falling material. I am sure by then Jesus stops preaching. They look up again. This time there are four faces staring down at the worshippers. Just then, the one who couldn't find a way in is lowered into the very center of the church, right in the front row. Quite a story, don't you think? How hard is it, anyway, for all the diversity of humankind to find easy entrance into the church; to be welcomed and accepted for no matter who you are, no matter what you do, no matter where one is in one's faith or life journey? Transformation begins with vision. Vision is the fuel that drives it all.

A new vision which stays hidden under a bushel basket will contribute very little to the transformation of a church. Like the familiar spiritual says: "This little light of mine, I'm gonna let it shine. Everywhere I go, I'm gonna let it shine. All through the night, I'm gonna let it shine." A visible, communicated, and understood vision is where bringing a dying church back to life begins. But there also needs to be a plan to carry out the vision. What is the next step? How are we going to get from here to there? What is the road that needs to be traveled to bridge the gap between reality and vision? The new vision for Middle Church was big; the plan to carry it out was simple: it needed to be repeated, repeated, repeated; rehearsed, rehearsed, rehearsed; taught, taught, taught; and modeled, modeled, modeled. The vision needed to be repeated, rehearsed and modeled in one-on-one conversations; in groups, programs, sermons, the arts, worship planning, outreach into the community, church school, prayers, education, and announcements. There are hundreds of ways in the regular worship, life, ministry and outreach of the church in which the vision can be communicated verbally as well as nonverbally through the use of the arts. "Always, in everything said and done, stay on message. Leaders do not worry about redundancy. Just when someone cannot bear the thought of saying the same things yet another time, most people are just beginning to take it in. Redundancy is essential, though effective communicators find new ways to tell the same story."[7] Through intentional and constant communication and modeling, in time, the new transforming vision will become systemic and natural to the church, a part of its very essence and existence. No longer will the church be a static, declining church, but a transformed/transforming church with a new vision of life and hope. Discovering a vision for a church is not a one-time thing. Repeating, rehearsing, and modeling the vision are essential to the process. Many vision statements read and sound terrific, but putting them into action can be quite adventurous and even filled with unanticipated problems and distractions.

---

[7] Weems, *Take the Next Step,* p. 120

Chapter Four

A Problem with the Vision
Everybody says welcome

I thought the vision was clear. It made sense. It seemed doable. What before was complex now seemed quite understandable. But it didn't take long to discover that there was a fundamental problem with the vision. The vision was to continuously open more doors, persistently create more entry points, and constantly welcome more and a greater diversity of people. The problem was with the word "welcome." Everybody uses the word welcome. It is the easiest word in the English language to say, write, print, and display on a bulletin board or banner, but the hardest word on the planet to do. And now, diversity, multiculturalism and multiracialism are becoming similar "in" phrases—easy to say and claim; hard to do and maintain.

Welcome. Welcome. Welcome. Wherever you go, you read it on outside bulletin boards, on the front cover of worship programs, and in church advertisements and brochures. You hear it from friendly and enthusiastic greeters at the front doors of nearly every church. Outside a small town in rural Pennsylvania, there is a church with a large cemetery in front of it and the church sign planted in the middle of the cemetery proudly displays the word "welcome." Welcome. What do we mean? The next time you go to a church or a public gathering, ask that question and the greeters will often become suddenly inarticulate or smile and quickly move on to welcome someone else or look at you like you are stupid. "What do you mean, what is welcome? Everybody knows it means just what it says—everybody is welcome." Sure it does.

People of color are welcome. Is the paid and volunteer leadership in the church all white? Is the worship to which people of color are invited all European in content and style? Is the music of the church mainly by white European composers who died four hundred years ago? Are there people of color elected or appointed to the official board of the church and participants in the decision-making process? What does it mean to welcome?

Gay men and lesbian women are welcome. Are there gay and lesbian persons in the upfront paid and volunteer leadership of the church? May gays and lesbians participate as couples and be treated as families in the life and worship of the church? Does the church only offer and celebrate events, ceremonies, anniversaries, and marriages for the heterosexual persons in the congregation? Do we quote the Bible only when a literal interpretation agrees with whom we want in or out of the church? What does it mean to welcome?

Women are welcome. Are there women in the upfront paid, volunteer, and decision-making leadership of the church? Are there women holding senior clergy and church leadership positions? Does the church use sexist or inclusive language? Are women a real part of the team or simply consigned to child-care, friendship hour, or children's ministry add-ons? What does it mean to welcome?

The same questions need to be asked about other cultures, a variety of family structures, children, performing and fine artists, etc. What does it mean to welcome? It means just exactly what it says, everybody is welcome! Sure it does.

In a sermon at Glide Memorial Church in San Francisco, the Reverend Cecil Williams said, "Whose time is it now? Is it somebody else's time? Whose time is it? It is God's time. And it's God's people's time. And God's people are everybody. It's everybody's time. It's all of our time. So, it seems to me, we've got to do what we've got to do to make it everybody's time. As people of faith, what we've got to do is to discover the 'practice of Jesus' in our lives. In other words, to learn to practice what we believe."

Welcome means everything needs to change. Everything. Wesley Granberg-Michaelson observes when a new vision is discovered to transform a stagnant, declining, or dying church, there are "two anxieties: The first is a nagging fear that in the end, despite the fine words and rhetoric, nothing in the organization will ever really change. But second is the destabilizing anxiety over the fact that indeed, everything— yes actually everything—will change!"[8]

One of the major problems with discovering a fresh vision to bring new life to a congregation is that too many church leaders and boards separate welcome and diversity. If transformation includes "everything must change" and "everything must change" includes "everybody welcome," then transfor-

---

[8] Wesley Granberg-Michaelson, *Leadership From Inside Out: Spirituality and Organizational Change,* (The Crossroad Publishing Company, New York), p. 110.

mation, change, welcome, and diversity cannot be separated. Several years ago I was invited to participate in a diversity planning session for a seminary in the Midwest. At one point, participants were divided into small groups to discuss possible diversity strategies for the seminary which each group would share with the larger gathering later in the day. Our unit began with a time of introductions and personal sharing. Then a member of the group, who was a student at the seminary, started the discussion by saying she did not see the real need for the gathering because the seminary was already diverse—everybody is welcome here. To illustrate the welcoming, diverse environment of the seminary, she said the student body included several women as well as a number of persons from a sister denomination. A polite discussion followed.

I sat back in my chair uncharacteristically speechless. My understanding of diversity was so unlike what was being discussed that I didn't know where to enter into the conversation. Diversity, like the words welcome and multicultural, is used so broadly today that it can mean something radically different to different people and groups and in different cultures and environments. When I use the word diversity in a workshop or at a conference, I often notice people nodding their heads affirmatively. Of course everybody is welcome in our church. Of course our church affirms diversity. Of course we encourage our church to be multicultural and multiracial. That's what church is. That's what the church does. That's why we have greeters at the front doors on Sunday mornings. That's why we display on our outside bulletin board, "Everybody Welcome." But I know many people do not mean the same thing I do when I use the words welcome and diversity.

I am passionately committed to diversity. There is another minister in New York City who rarely greets me by my name, but instead by "Minister of Diversity." Minister of Diversity—I like that name, but it's a hard one to live up to. Unlike multicultural, diversity is a broad term and can mean many things. Diversity is more than black and white, male and female. This is why, when we use the term, it is helpful to list exactly what we mean. It is a bit awkward, but it does clarify the meaning upfront. Diversity means we welcome members regardless of race, culture, sexual-orientation, gender, age, economic status, skills, talent, physically challenged, belief, and religion. And that doesn't even exhaust the diverse possibilities within a human gathering such as a congregation. We need to be careful when we talk about diversity, especially if what we really mean is multicultural and multiracial. It can be a conflicting term. We want our church to be a diverse church. Do we, really? We want the broader community to know that our place is a place of diversity—all are welcome here. Are they, really?

Like welcome, diversity means everything must change. I am not talking about what is a popular practice today, which is to include one person of color on the board and call the church a diverse, multiracial church. That's called "look good" diversity, and is very different from systemic diversity. We cannot call ourselves a diverse, welcoming, including congregation and at the same time expect everybody to adapt to exactly the way we currently are in our worship, programs, education, and ministry. Worship will change. Music will change. Leadership will change. Programs will change. Educational opportunities will change. The official board will change. Administration will change. The way we do things will change. The way we look will change. Who we are will change. Ministry will change. Outreach will change. The systemic essence and essential identity of the church will change.

Diversity is both dangerous and exciting. It is celebratory and also very hard work. We should not use the words welcome and diversity too lightly or quickly, especially if we don't really mean it or if we don't intend to change anything.

Like many things that are important, diversity, multiculturalism, multiracialism, and creating other new diverse entry points into the church won't happen unless they are intentional. They will not happen if transformational leaders do not lead the way to make them happen. Transformation begins with a new vision which must be accompanied by a clear plan to carry out the vision.

Discovering a new vision of a welcoming, diverse congregation is not only exciting and adventuresome, but is in the congregation's best ministry, worship and growth interest. It is difficult. The impact can be challenging and may even involve uncovering unconscious prejudices and leading a congregation through some unpleasant realities. Diversity, like welcome, is a great word and a desirable goal, but it is not easy to be, do, and even harder to sustain over time. To be welcoming and diverse, all members, participants, and visitors must feel they are included and accepted for who they are and for what they can contribute as persons. It is up to all the paid and volunteer leaders to lead the way in celebrating, welcoming, and including all the persons, talents, cultures, races, sexual orientations, genders, ages, and personal contributions within the congregation. The goal is for welcoming, diversity, multiculturalism, and multiracialism to become natural, systemic parts of the worship, life, ministry, administration, and spirit of the church. Anything less is not the Gospel. Anything less is only "look good" change, not transformation. "In the final analysis change sticks only when it becomes 'the way we do things here,' when it seeps into the very bloodstream of the work unit or corporate body. Until new behaviors are rooted in social norms and shared values, they are always subject to degradation as soon as the pressures associated with a change are removed."[9] If transformational leaders will lead, there is nothing to be afraid of.

In the Gospel by Mark there is a story about Jesus and his disciples in a boat crossing Lake Galilee. Suddenly, a wind begins to stir up the waves. Water spills over the sides into the boat. The disciples are terrified. Jesus is sleeping. "Teacher," they yell, "do you not care that we are perishing out here; do you not care that we are afraid and scared of what may happen to us?" In one of the most incredible biblical scenes, Jesus awakes, stands up, remains calm, and simply says to the lake: "Peace." The water is still. His disciples look at one another and say, "Whew! Did you see that? Who is this in the boat with us, that even the wind and the sea obey him?" Who is this? Ah, now we finally come to the very heart and soul of Mark's good news. Who is this? Who are we? Who are the mosaic of people that are the community, the town, the city? Who are the many peoples and nations of the world? Why is it so difficult to answer and respond to that question? Who is this? This is the Beloved One with whom God is well pleased. And that question begs another: Who are we? We, all of God's grand diversity, are the beloved ones with whom God is very well pleased. Anything less is not the Gospel. Who is this? God's Beloved One, who is capable of welcoming, embracing, caring, including, and responding. Who are we? Can it be Gospel? Could it be Gospel? Is it true? Can it be true? Is it possible to believe that no matter

---

[9] John P. Kotter, *Leading Change,* (Harvard Business School Press, Boston, Massachusetts), P. 14.

who, no matter what, no matter the condition, no matter the circumstances, no matter where we are in our faith or life journeys, we are God's beloved ones, capable of welcoming, embracing, caring, including, and responding. Who is this? God's Beloved One. Who are we? God's beloved ones. What an incredible story! Can it be that anything less is not Gospel? Is it possible that anything less is not Gospel? If transformational leaders will lead, there is nothing to be afraid of. Sometimes leadership that changes a chaotic environment is as simple as saying "yes."

Chapter Five

Just Say Yes
How simple is that?

When our granddaughter, Mabel, was two years old, she loved to say "no" and wouldn't say "yes" unless there were no other options available for her to get something she really wanted. One of my favorite games with her was to look into her eyes and say "yes." She would look at me with a mischievous smile and reply "no." And the game was on: "yes," "no," "yes," "no," "yes," "no," until I finally gave up. She eventually grew out of that and we now play different games.

There are some church leaders who either never grow out of saying "no" or who just can't get themselves to say "yes" to someone else's good or potentially good idea. To just say "yes" is a critical leadership quality that positively encourages the transformation, growth, and diversity of a congregation. Some of Middle's most important programs came into being by simply saying "yes." Jerriese, a gay African-American Middle Church member, elder, and a professional performer, asked if he could start a gospel choir. He talked about his vision and how he didn't sense much enthusiasm when he approached others with his idea. The answer was "yes" and the East Village Gospel Choir was created. It played a critical role in the early transformation, growth and diversity of the congregation. Middle's commitment was to Jerriese and the choir. When he was ill from complications with HIV/AIDS, he frequently mentioned a fear of not being remembered. I assured him that would never happen on my watch. When he died in 1995, I ended his memorial by renaming the choir the Jerriese Johnson East Village Gospel Choir.

In the mid-to-late 1980s, many arts programs were cut or severely diminished in the public schools on the Lower East Side and in the East Village of New York City. Lyn, a community activist, an adjunct faculty at New York University, a member of Middle Church, and a deacon on the church's board proposed the establishment of an after school arts center for elementary school children. The answer was "yes" and the Middle Collegiate Church Children's AfterSchool Arts Center was created, providing movement, crafts, theater, photography, pottery, and homework assistance for the neighborhood children. The after school program also provided an important outreach to area parents, offered quality arts experience and education for neighborhood children, and established a significant connection between the church and the community. It was a key "open door" into the church and into the community from the church.

In 1986, early in the discovery of HIV/AIDS and in a time when there were a lot of myths and fears about the disease and how it spread, Ed walked into the church house unannounced and asked if he could speak with me. He shared how he wanted to do something important for people with HIV/AIDS in the East Village. He went from church to church seeking a partner, but was turned down after every request. Middle, he said, was his last stop. His proposal was to serve a meal, distribute groceries and vegetables, and provide basic services. His vision was to think of the meal as a form of Holy Communion, spiritual as well as physical, based upon the biblical stories of Jesus sharing food, love, and compassion with others. To him, the very act of sharing food with people in need was a holy act. The answer was "yes" and the pioneering Celebrate Life Meal for Persons Living with HIV/AIDS was created. Every Monday night a meal was served, vegetables and groceries were distributed, people were greeted and hugged, a social worker, nurse, and nutritionist were available, entertainment was provided, and special event parties were planned, all this from just saying "yes." The Celebrate Life Meal, which served over one hundred people, was an inspiring program and an incredible witness that reached out to the entire city of New York and became the subject of numerous articles and videos.

Wendy, a member of Middle Church, a photographer, and a photo editor of a magazine, approached me about creating a photo gallery and dark room in Middle's church house. The answer was "yes" and the Middle Collegiate Church Gallery and dark room were created. Peter, a member of Middle Church and a builder, made and hung display cases in Middle's social hall. Every month a new show was opened with a gala reception, and another "entry door" swung open into Middle Church and out toward the community.

There are so many other stories that tell of so many other entry doors opened through which people entered into the ministry, life, and worship of Middle Church. Middle was resurrected, grew, and became hugely diverse, often challenged and encouraged by first just saying "yes." For a church that was stagnant and dying for so long, saying "yes" was refreshing to members, participants, and to the wider community and created many new and thriving programs and events. The answer "yes" can have an incredibly uplifting effect upon a declining and depressed church. I will never understand why "yes" is such a difficult word for so many church leaders to say and to do. Along with "intentional," "yes" is another important word in a transformational leader's vocabulary.

Much of the confidence and faith that allowed Middle's board and me to just say yes to so many people's different suggestions, ideas, and assistance came from Ezekiel's timeless story of the valley of dry bones. To respond positively to a person's potentially good proposal had the surprising power to lift up my own spirit, refresh my vision, and point me in a positive direction. Ezekiel's story did that for me and for the congregation. No other story in the Bible so visually describes how we or our congregations may sometimes feel—stagnant, dysfunctional, lifeless, so little spirit and energy, declining, dying like dry bones. At many critical moments, God asks us and we ask God and one another, "Can these dry bones live again; can persons, relationships, institutions, churches, communities, nations, and the environment live again? Can these bones come back to life?" Faith's answer is: "Sure they can. Sure they can. No bones about it." I believe that.

I attended a worship celebration at a church in a small community in New Jersey. During a conversation following the worship, one person identified herself as a clergyperson who was visiting the church for the first time. While walking out of the church, I noticed she was also leaving. I stopped and introduced myself. She looked surprised and replied, "Gordon Dragt. I know you. You were the presenter at a conference I once attended. You are the 'can-these-dry-bones-live-again-sure-they-can-sure-they-can-minister.'" Yup, that's me, alright, and to just say yes is one intentional action that helps make it happen.

A transformed/transforming church is characterized by professional and volunteer leaders who feel called, are grounded in an appropriate vision, are intentional and up to the challenge of carrying out the vision, and are not afraid of saying "yes." Another critical characteristic of a church that is purposefully changing from declining to thriving is the multi-cultural and multiracial commitment of its leaders. For me, this commitment centers in the life and legacy of Dr. Martin Luther King, Jr.

Chapter Six

Influenced by Dr. Martin Luther King, Jr.
Never again

"Dr. Martin Luther King, Jr. Sunday" was always one of the first entries in my church planning calendar. It had as much importance in the worship and ministry of the church as Christmas, Easter, and Pentecost. Dr. King was one of our nation's most prominent leaders and preachers who, decades ago, literally turned my life around and radically changed every aspect of my ministry. People often asked me how I became so committed to creating a multicultural, multiracial church and so passionately focused upon diversity and welcoming all of God's beautiful rainbow of peoples into the life, worship, and ministry of the church—no questions asked, no requirements needed, no invitations necessary. The answer was simple: the application was difficult, intentional, and constant. It is what Dr. King called "The Beloved Community." "The goal," he said, "is reconciliation, the goal is redemption, the goal is the creation of the beloved community."[10]

Every year in January on Dr. Martin Luther King, Jr. Sunday, I am reminded that when Dr. King was assassinated in 1968, I was a young minister who had grown up in a small farming community in southwestern Michigan. I was ordained for only three years and served a new church start which had begun in a mostly white suburban Bucks County, Pennsylvania community. Dr. King's grand vision was for all of God's beautiful rainbow of peoples to live, worship, play, and work together in dignity, justice, community, and equality; for the diversity of the earth's peoples and nations to exist together as sisters and brothers; and for a peaceful and nonviolent end to the tragic injustice of war. This imposing vision of the beloved community, which was forged out of an environment of violence, fear, and hate, passionately transformed my own vision, radically changed me forever, and fundamentally altered the whole focus and energy of my personal spirituality and public ministry. Never again, I promised myself. Never again would I ever be a minister in a mono-cultural, mono-racial church. Never again. After the death of Dr. King, I never looked at the church the same again. I never looked at society and government leaders the same again. I never looked at scripture the same again. I never looked at leadership the same again. I never looked at myself the same again. I never looked at my past the same again. I never looked at ministry the same again. Never again.

Without understanding Dr. King's vision of the beloved community, I cannot fully understand who I am or why I do things the way I do or why I read the Bible the way I do or why I believe certain things so passionately or why I am so

---

[10] Cf. Dr. Martin Luther King, Jr.'s 1957 speech, *Birth of a New Nation*.

enthusiastically committed to the possibility of the church to be a special place of diversity, welcome, and acceptance. The prophets called it the peaceable reign of God on earth. Jesus talked about it in his famous prayer, God, Your will be done (where?), here on earth, here in suburban Bucks County, here in the city of New York, here in the East Village, as it is in heaven. The Apostles called it the new creation. Dr. Martin Luther King, Jr. called it the beloved community.

The next Sunday following Dr. King's assassination, I looked out at this developing Bucks County, Pennsylvania congregation. It was all white. Never again. This is not the way God's beloved community looks. Transformation has to be intentional or it won't happen. Mono-culturalism and mono-racialism are what automatically happen. Transformation of a church doesn't take place simply by a person announcing from the pulpit that she or he thinks it is a good idea to change. Multicultural, multiracial congregations are developed intentionally, and cannot be sustained until the very essence and essential identity of the congregation is diverse, multicultural, and multiracial.

From that time on, worship in this new church start changed. Music changed. Worship leadership changed. Sermons changed. Relationships with a Philadelphia-based African-American cultural center and an African-American dance ensemble were established. We participated in each other's gatherings and celebrations. We advertised widely and purposefully, and articles regarding the congregation's diversity began appearing in Bucks County and Philadelphia papers. A broader group of persons began to attend, both from the local area and from the wider Philadelphia metropolitan region. The face and spirit of the congregation changed.

Some folks in the community liked what they saw; others

didn't. On one Sunday, a neighbor stood at the fence between her property and the church building yelling through a battery powered megaphone at people attending the worship, "This is not a church, it's nigger heaven." We did not retaliate or retreat. Instead we intensified our efforts. If racism can be institutionalized, so can anti-racism. We increased efforts to transform the congregation with local multiracial concerts, multiracial theater productions in school auditoriums that challenged the audiences, and a broader participation of people of color in the life, worship, decision-making, and leadership of the church. The church became one of the most diverse congregations in the predominately white suburban Bucks County region.

The Dr. Martin Luther King, Jr. Holiday highlights what is still the most critical issue of our time, which is to learn how to live together. In a speech in The Riverside Church in New York City, Dr. King challenged the church to wake up from its ethical, moral, faith, and biblical slumber when he said the eleven-o'clock hour on Sunday mornings is one of the most segregated times in America. This is not the beloved community envisioned for the church. There are always opportunities to nurture diversity, open more doors, and create more entry points. Every year on the King Holiday, it is important for church leaders to repeat the meaning and importance of the beloved community. The beloved community is about all people having opportunities to experience worshipping, living, and loving one another. It is about the church being passionate and intentional about modeling the diverse beloved community. It is about the growing diversity of our society. If diversity has not already happened where you are, be prepared, because it is coming to your town, your rural community, and your suburbia, soon. Multiculturalism is not just a city experience; it is a national and global fact. It is the present face of most of the communities and will be the future face of all the communities. Learning how to live together is the most important issue of our time—locally, regionally, nationally and globally. If diversity, multiculturalism, and multiracialism cannot be experienced in our churches, then where? For the future of the church, we can no longer tolerate the eleven-o'clock hour to be the most segregated time in our nation. It is not the Gospel. It is not the beloved community. It does not contribute to the vitality and growth of the church. Never again.

God blessed life with a vivid diversity. Very few things can more authentically turn around a static and declining church than positively embracing God's blessing. Systemic diversity, along with the arts, a welcoming vision, and outreach into the community are essential ingredients to church resurrection and growth.

Chapter Seven

Basic Church Mathematics
I can smell a plateau coming

To reinvent a dysfunctional, declining, or near dead church, there are not only the many difficult internal and systemic changes that must occur, but attention also needs to be given to the church's external dimensions and growth. Church growth has both internal and external components. For transformation to be systemic and long lasting, attention needs to be given to both of these important considerations. The external component of congregational transformation is basic church mathematics, which includes two important dynamics.

The first dynamic is to keep adding; let subtraction happen naturally. A close relative to saying "yes" is to regularly add new programs, open new doors, and create new entry points into the church from the community and into the community from the church. In a time of transformation and change, don't cut old programs. Let old programs that don't fit the constantly evolving vision die a natural death. To cut long-standing, once cherished programs when trying to transform a congregation may simply raise the tension level too high and cause unnecessary distractions or detours from the main goal. To let no-longer-relevant programs die a graceful death will allow the tension level to remain manageable and help the leaders and congregation to remain focused on the new vision with fewer unnecessary diversions.

When I started at Middle Church, the most active church group was the Women's Guild. Some of its members were also the most passionate guardians of the past. I was quite sure a Women's Guild was not going to be included in the new vision of a resurrected Middle. Women's ministry would look quite different. But these older women were currently the core of what was left of the congregation. It was their church, not mine. To cut the group would have caused even more chaos than what already existed and would have created a long complicated distraction from moving forward with the new vision. Instead, I became an active member of the Women's Guild. I paid my dues and was the first official male member in it's over one-hundred-and-fifty-year history. I took my turn providing refreshments after the meetings. I never missed a meeting and was always included on the agenda to give a report of what was currently happening at Middle and what was being planned for the future. At each meeting, members of the Women's Guild were given an opportunity to share their opinions, give feedback, and voice their concerns and opposition. Over time, some of the women became the greatest early cheerleaders for the new vision to transform and grow their church. As a younger and much more diverse group of people became participants and members of the new congregation, they didn't take part in the Women's Guild activities. Women's ministry at Middle went in a completely different direction, but the new people loved, cherished, and celebrated the presence of the older women in the congregation and the reverse was also true. Eventually, all these beloved women died and the Women's Guild died a natural death, too. Even though none of them were persons of means, they all left in their wills modest gifts to their church, which was a way of saying thanks for including them, not bypassing them, in the miracle that happened at Second Avenue and 7th Street.

The second external dynamic of basic church mathematics is to respond to membership and participation decline proactively, not retroactively. I can smell a plateau coming. Several years ago I led a clergy retreat on the topic of injecting new life into the local congregation. At one point I talked about the Middle experience of resurrecting a declining city church of just a few members into a vibrant church of several hundred members. During a discussion that followed, one of the ministers said he had been at his current church for fifteen years and the membership had declined from around a hundred and fifty to about fifty. He felt my emphasis upon external, numerical growth was basically saying his ministry was a failure. Another minister responded with a similar story, except he added that even though the church's membership remained small, they had experienced considerable internal, spiritual growth. He, too, felt my excitement about growing a church by increasing members and participants diminished the success he had over the years in growing his stable, albeit externally stagnant, congregation inwardly and spiritually. I understand these criticisms and I also understand that church growth is not just about either/or, but both/and.

Many stagnant or dying churches have been this way for so long that they develop a small church mentality and settle-in comfortably with the status quo. That wasn't the way it was with Middle, although the end result was the same. Middle had a big church mentality with a dying church reality. The handful of people still active participated in an imaginary church that didn't exist and had not existed for at least thirty years. I have seen too many churches in too many vital locations become and remain small and ineffective, unable to connect with the constantly evolving neighborhood around them, and incapable of maintaining a relevant life, ministry, and mission year after year after year. What is this about? Where is the leadership? I was never ashamed of talking about giving proper attention to the external components of church growth. I was never embarrassed talking about the importance of growing a church numerically. It is one significant component of transforming a church. I am a progressive/liberal clergyperson who has never been embarrassed to call himself an evangelist. I am an evangelist. I was never bashful about it. I believe it is biblical. You don't have to be a conservative or evangelical or whatever to talk about church growth, evangelism, and mission. It is a fundamental responsibility of our calling into the ministry to be missional. What's up with so many progressive/liberal church leaders who are embarrassed to talk about numbers and about the biblical imperative to expand the church's mission, membership, and participation? Too many clergy convince themselves and their boards that it is enough to grow spiritually or inwardly while the numbers remain static or continue in slow decline.

I fully understand the place and ministry of the small church in our culture and the excellent material and examples of the emerging church concept. But it is obvious I am not the one to make the case for the small or emerging church. Others are more qualified and experienced to do that and have much more enthusiasm for the topic. I have, however, seen my share of churches that remain small because their vision, mission, imagination, energy, and attitude remain small. For me, that is a faith and leadership problem. I cannot help myself. I just think, believe, and act this way. It is a systemic part of my spiritual DNA. When I drive, ride, or walk through a vital community which appears to have potential, and I see wonderful church facilities with tiny congregations, I wonder why more people are not attracted to them. I almost always say to myself, "Give me three-to-five years and I could resurrect that place into an internally/externally growing, festive congregation." You may call it arrogant, but I call it faith, calling, ministry, vision, mission, and leadership. It's just basic church mathematics.

I hate plateaus in my personal life, and I hated them even more in the life and worship of the church. I became restless when the church membership and worship attendance became static for too long. I made quick and adaptive moves if there was even a brief period of decline. I sometimes intentionally aggravated the staff at Middle Collegiate Church by beginning our meetings with the statement, "I can smell a plateau coming." And I could. It was just who I was. I could smell a plateau coming in new membership meetings and in worship attendance long before it actually arrived. The staff always predictably replied by telling me what I already knew—the last new member class was one of our largest ever and worship attendance remained at a record level. I knew that, but I could smell a plateau coming. I encouraged all the church staff and leaders to be more intentional, more focused, more creative and imaginative, to reach out broader, to stretch their arms out wider, and to keep opening more doors and creating more entry points into the church from the community and into the community from the church. It is always more fun and rewarding to be proactive instead of reactive.

One of the quick fixes for static or declining membership and worship attendance that boards of churches like to propose is to contact all the people who have left the church and invite them to come back and participate in the church's transformation. It sounds like a good, even compassionate thing to do, and it may even get some short-term results for the temporary revitalization of a congregation. But to spend energy and time looking backward is a big-time distraction if the goal is to systemically change and transform the congregation with a new vision for a new life and ministry. A better transformational strategy is to let go of those who have left and concentrate upon welcoming and building the new congregation that will come. To be aware that the resurrection of a church may cause loss is difficult and painful, but sometimes necessary to move forward.

Several years ago, I arrived early at a wedding and had an opportunity to talk with some of the guests before the celebration was scheduled to begin. At one point I was introduced to a guest as "the minister." He immediately entered into a lengthy conversation about the church in which he was an active member. Normally, I try to avoid such long conversations and make every effort to circulate more, but I was interested in the story the person told me.

He said his church was rapidly declining, so in a three-month process they set out to discover a new vision and direction. Out of this vision, they developed a one-year plan to increase worship attendance and membership. To help them reach their goal, they did extensive advertising and promotion in the community. "So far," he said, "we are on target. It looks like we are going to meet our goal."

Then, without any prompting on my part, he made an incredible observation: "The real surprise," he said, "was not that our worship attendance increased and that we got some new members, but what we didn't take into consideration when we talked about a new vision and a plan to accomplish it, was that welcoming new persons into our church would also mean welcoming who they are and their ideas and different ways of doing things. We didn't plan for that. Today, I tell you, our church isn't anything like it used to be. That was a real surprise. We've grown, all right; some like it and some don't; some long-time members stayed and some left. I think you have to be careful what you ask for."

In my entire active ministry, I intentionally set out to prove wrong the traditional church growth idea that churches grow best by attracting like people. There are many ways to grow a church. I've served churches in a small town, suburbia, large town, and in the heart of the largest city in the nation. Every one of them grew numerically by intentionally becoming diverse, multiple-entry-point congregations. Churches need to look more like the people and the society we serve, and all our cities, towns and suburbia are becoming increasingly diverse. You may not notice it in our churches, but some Sunday morning go to the local Home Depot or Shop Rite and you will see what I'm talking about. The parking lots are full and the aisles are a beehive of multicultural energy. It is important for transformational leaders to intentionally reach out, relate, welcome, be relevant, make meaningful space for, and include the whole diverse community around them. If it isn't done intentionally, it won't happen. It's just basic church mathematics.

An essential component of basic church mathematics is to first discover the church's new vision, and then develop a plan to communicate that vision in every way available. A church's budget needs to include a comprehensive communication line item that will consist of, among other things, newspaper advertising, web site development and maintenance, newsletters, brochures, handouts, posters, and so-on. Communication is evangelism; it is reaching out into the broader community with a message and an invitation. But be careful. Make sure the communication says what you do and you do what it says. Especially for churches, truth in advertising is important. A negative effect will result if people read an ad in the newspaper or check out the web site, like what they read and see, then come to church during a Sunday worship celebration and discover their experience does not live up to what was promised. 1010WIN Radio in New York has a relevant slogan: "If we're not saying what you're seeing, let us know."

In 1996 *The New York Times* printed a nearly full-page article about Middle's worship, life, and ministry. The headline was: "Middle Collegiate Church, Where Old Time Religion Gets Some New Twists." The article talked about bringing the dying church back to life and described some of the exciting things included in the Sunday worship celebrations. The piece appeared in the Friday edition. When I took another look at the worship celebration planned for the next Sunday, I didn't think it lived up to the exciting description in the article. I immediately called two other staff members and we made some quick changes in Sunday's worship. At our next staff meeting we had a long discussion about how, from now on, all Sundays need to be special Sundays; no Sunday could ever again be considered regular or ordinary. We needed to be especially alert to do what we said and to only say what we actually did.

The next Sunday, two days after the article appeared in *The New York Times*, we estimated approximately one hundred and fifty more people attended the worship celebration than attended the previous week. We were determined not to let God, the people, and Middle Church down, and we were determined to keep as many of these new people as possible coming back to Middle. That meant we needed to take care that the Middle experience for these new people matched what was said about Middle. The same principle is true for everything and in everyway a church communicates.

When I retired and moved to a new community, I checked out the newspaper advertisements and web sites of most of the local churches. The first thing I discovered was that many of the advertisements appeared to be routine, not very creative, and, quite frankly, boring. I assumed the churches were the same. Some of the ads only listed the sermon title. I didn't care about that. I wanted to get a glimpse of the spirit or the essence of the church. There were two ads that did communicate what I was looking for. On the basis of that information, I immediately deleted one from my "church to visit list" and placed the other one at the top of the list. A few of the web sites were even more disappointing than the newspaper ads. Many proved to be completely lacking reality, some were hopelessly out of date and obviously non-maintained—in July one was still advertising the previous Christmas celebrations—but a couple were creative, well-maintained, informative, and inviting. When I attended a church, I always perused the available brochures and literature with interest. That was also a mixed experience. Quality is important. But even more important is that a visitor can detect very quickly if a church has a clear mission and a vision to accomplish it. Without a clear discovered vision, a church's communication is hollow and will probably never mirror reality.

There is a lot of church shopping going on today, but not all clergy and church leaders are aware of it. It takes place behind a computer screen at home, in a café, or at work. It was my practice at new member meetings to always ask how each participant first heard about Middle Church. Word of mouth from a friend, a colleague at work, or in a conversation at a party, of course, was always a big reason behind people visiting a church. But as the "word of mouth folks" got home, they soon checked out the church on the internet. Others browsed the internet because they decided to begin going to church again or they moved and wanted to attend a church in their new community. They often went to the internet first and checked out the web sites of the area churches. That's the current equivalent of church shopping. Quality and maintained web sites are important. Don't even think about resurrecting a stagnant, declining, or dying church without one. It is an essential tool for doing basic church mathematics.

Outreach into the community from the church is another critical component of the basic mathematics of transforming and growing a church. A church without an important major outreach effort is not attractive today. It is as simple as that. People are not only concerned with their own spiritual well-being and life journeys, but also interested in the spiritual and physical well-being of others. If a church wants to attract new persons, grow, and be transformed from a static or declining existence, it needs to establish at least one or two meaningful outreach ministries. Some people want to be involved in these ministries personally, others only minimally, and still others only want to proudly tell their friends and colleagues how their church actively reaches out and makes a significant contribution to the spiritual and physical life of the neighbor-hood and beyond. Outreach efforts will definitely bring some new twists and challenges to the life of a congregation and will add new participants and members. This is, after all, what the church should be doing anyway.

Early at Middle Collegiate Church we recognized the fundamental importance of the outreach component of basic church mathematics. We made a commitment to establish several significant outreach efforts that met important needs in the community and the city. One of the most visionary was the Celebrate Life Meal for People Living with HIV/AIDS, which began in 1987 when the illness began to become an epidemic and people were afraid of catching it from kitchen sinks, water fountains, and bathroom toilets. We also started a Clothes Closet which distributed clothing and a Food Pantry that gave out groceries for persons in temporary need of these necessities. An affordable and quality five-day Children's AfterSchool Arts Center served neighborhood children, many of whom came from single parent homes. A children's arts camp, which used the entire city for tours and outings, was available for the summer months. Space was rented inexpensively to a variety of performing arts groups and on Tuesday and Saturday nights several hundred people attended AA gatherings. An eight-block Second Avenue Street Festival raised funds for HIV/AIDS ministries, increased AIDS awareness within the community and the city, and provided opportunities for HIV/AIDS service groups in the city to network with one another. A senior adult center was created to give neighborhood seniors an opportunity for social contact and provide basic personal, nutritional, recreational, educational, and referral services. A multicultural, multiracial, multi-sexual orientation East Village Gospel Choir sang on scheduled Sundays and at events throughout the city. People were invited to sing in the choir without audition and without being members of Middle Church. It served a musical, social, and spiritual purpose for the participants. A social worker was on staff, mostly to assist with the many needs of area senior adults and people with HIV/AIDS. A yearly neighborhood festival was established, to which all of the social service organizations in the East Village and the Lower East Side were invited. The festival gave the many organizations an opportunity to network with one another and the community an opportunity to have conversation and/or volunteer with groups in which they were interested. As a part of our outreach efforts, Middle supported a variety of community groups, including: the Lower East Side Girl's Club, East Village Visiting Neighbors, children's daycare and nursery school programs, HIV/AIDS service organizations, national and international relief projects, affordable housing efforts, ecumenical organizations and events, artists and arts organizations. We networked with United Way, the local UPS drivers, and a regional foundation to assist in funding a variety of outreach efforts to community children and families. Outreach is a fundamental component of basic church mathematics and stretching out into the community from the church is what Middle did; it was a part of the "essential spirit of Middle," and it had a positive effect upon bringing a dead church back to life. Outreach is a non-negotiable component of basic transformational church mathematics.

Still another significant component of basic church mathematics in bringing new life to a congregation concerns the minister's and the church's denominational relationship. I am an ordained and supportive minister in the Reformed Church in America, but at Middle we didn't make a big deal about our denominational identity. It was my experience that most people searched for and attended a church that best fit their own spiritual needs and journeys, not because of its denominational affiliation. The new Middle congregation attracted people from many different church and non-church backgrounds. Middle's unity was its diversity, not its denomination. Basic church mathematics has many different components and they all contribute to bringing new life to a dying church.

One component important to church vitality that will be covered in much greater depth in future chapters is the use of the arts in the total life, worship and ministry of the church. Chapter Eight begins the discussion with a story highlighting a common misunderstanding and potential problems with the arts and the church and includes a description of how the arts can be positive and indispensable partners for effective church transformation and growth. The chapter ends with challenging insights about the long and difficult task of creating systemic change in a congregation.

Chapter Eight

Early Struggle over Competing Visions
The arts – supported and celebrated in the church's total worship, life, and ministry

When I walked up the steps of Middle's church house to begin my ministry, I knew my charge was to resurrect a growing congregation with a vital ministry out of a nearly dead congregation, a mostly non-existent ministry, and a chaotic internal and external environment. A theater company, funded by Middle Church, was using space in the church house. My initial conversations with the leaders of the company were friendly and supportive, and I was looking forward to an exciting partnership that would be a great asset in growing the congregation and reaching out to the community. It didn't take me long, however, to discover that the theater literally occupied and controlled most of the church house and that any use of the space for programs and events I planned for purposes of growing the congregation needed to be adapted to their schedules. They existed with their own building use guidelines, had keys to the building and access to the rooms and offices, used the phones and equipment, and kept the schedules. The church office was also operated by the theater company and functioned mostly as their office. The only spaces available for me to use as a priority were my office on a full-time basis and the sanctuary, as long as it did not interfere with theater and dance performances in other places of the building. I was disappointed to discover that the company's vision for their theater, my position, the congregation, and the inclusion of the arts at Middle was quite different from my own vision. Since transforming Middle church also meant expanding the growing congregation's use of church house space for new programs, events, education, outreach, and small groups, conflict was inevitable with uncompromising tenants. What made the situation more difficult was that Middle's board supported the theater company's priority presence in the building, mostly out of a feeling of indebtedness to them for keeping the church house open, answering the phones, and protecting the building during a time when church leadership was non-existent or unable to lead and church programming was minimal. The theater company, of course, never tired of reminding anybody who would listen of that indebtedness.

It was obvious from the beginning that the board didn't want to confront the theater. They preferred to leave things as they were and avoid discussion of potential conflicts of mission and vision. They voiced, instead, that their most pressing and immediate concern was to attract new members and generate more income. I talked with them about how systemic change, not simply attracting more people and generating more income, was a main consideration. Sustained new life and growth was going to happen more through change and transformation than by re-vitalization or by doing even more of what it was already doing. The congregation and ministry had declined way too far and the community was changing way too rapidly for re-vitalization, avoidance, and inaction to be factors. It was going to take nothing less than complete transformation to bring this dead church back to life.

Right from the start I was in an uncomfortable position. I arrived with a twenty year history in a ministry of transforming and growing congregations through a celebration of the arts in the worship, life, and ministry of each congregation I served. Now, here I was, beginning a ministry in New York City in the heart of the East Village and already in a struggle with a theater company over conflicting visions for growing a dying congregation and how to establish an arts partnership in fulfilling that vision. It was awkward and I found myself in uncharted territory. I came to Middle to do what God called me to do and to fulfill the charge of my call, not to replay the dysfunction that had gone on before I arrived. My first efforts were toward supporting the company and providing artistic contacts and resources, but over time it was obvious that these efforts were not working. I was made very aware of just how difficult the struggle was going to be and how high the stakes were, when a leader of the theater company met me on the sidewalk outside the church house, looked me straight in the eye, and said: "You're an ambitious person, and I'm an ambitious person. For your own good, don't get in my way. Do I make myself clear?" He walked away and I just stood there. I had never experienced such a hostile situation before.

In a time when church leaders didn't lead, when the neighborhood was dramatically and quickly changing, the congregation was declining toward a probable death, and a vision for a new direction was not considered, the theater company came in and filled the gap. In the East Village of New York City space was a premium; free space was everything. In this leadership gap, Middle Church became a theater. There was a fundamental difference in vision and in practice between being a church with a theater or a theater with a church, and a church that celebrates, supports, encourages, and uses the arts in its total worship, life, and ministry. This was the vision of partnership with artists I needed to establish if I was to fulfill my charge to develop a vital, growing congregation at Middle Collegiate Church.

Eventually, an unpopular but increasingly obvious decision needed to be made to clear out the building and start over with a fresh vision of the arts providing the energy to grow a new Middle Church congregation, and to expand and diversify Middle's outreach and ministry. The timing of this decision was critical. For me to have tried earlier to move the theater company out on my own would have been a quick exit for me. To survive in this situation, I needed time to first give enough attention to "paying the rent," building up a new congregation, and encouraging new leaders and volunteers. The task of clearing the church house of its current occupants and starting over with a new vision wasn't easy or friendly. The theater company hired an attorney, went public in the community, lobbied Middle's board and the board of the Collegiate Church Corporation, and contacted New York City newspapers. The atmosphere between the theater and me became thick and tense. For the people of the theater company it was a real loss; for me it was painful and a time during which it was difficult to keep focused; for the Middle Church board it was a hard lesson learned about trust, leadership, vision, and partnerships. Times of transformation, change, and discovering and carrying out a new vision can be difficult, challenging, and even dangerous. I learned very quickly that I would be required to work harder in this ministry and to be more adaptive in my leadership than in any other ministry in the previous twenty years.

It took seven years to finally begin a fresh start at Middle Church—something only a survivor could have endured. Transformation of a chaotic and dysfunctional system can be a long and difficult process. Jim Herrington, in *Leading Congregational Change: A Practical Guide for the Transformational Journey*, says it takes three to five years to plant the seeds; five to seven years for the seeds to take root and begin to grow; seven to ten years for the plants to produce some buds; and ten years and beyond for the plants to blossom. That kind of lengthy process may be discouraging to some folks who like to "git 'er done" much quicker, but that is the plain talk about the realistic timeline for bringing systemic transformation to a stagnant, declining, or dying church. It is important to allow enough time for systemic change to take hold in the natural life and ministry of the church. Decline has a long head start on transformation. Persevere. "Perseverance is the indispensable competency for lasting change."[11] There are no shortcuts to major change. It takes time, sometimes much more time than we had ever anticipated. It took eleven years before Middle Collegiate Church became a dynamic, growing, constantly evolving, diverse, arts-friendly, multicultural, multiracial, multi-sexual orientation congregation. So if you are a clergy and you go to a church with the hopes of transforming and changing it into a vibrant new congregation and ministry, be prepared for a difficult, long, but ultimately satisfying and

---

[11] Weems, *Take the Next Step,* p. 143.

67

fulfilling ministry in that church. It won't happen short-term. There will happily be short-term gains, but systemic change takes longer. If you don't have what it takes to go the whole journey, don't go there. Try something else or somewhere else. It will only bring frustration to you and false hope to the congregation. That's the plain talk about being a transformational leader with the hope of resurrecting a dying church back to new life.

You may not have noticed this phrase in the middle of the chapter, "paying the rent." It only briefly appeared in a list with other important leadership tasks. Paying the rent, however, is so significant to what it means to be an adaptive, transformational leader, that the entire next chapter stories a discussion of this critical principle.

Chapter Nine

Paying the Rent
Build trust before making big changes

"A vision without execution is a hallucination."[12] The role of leader in recreating a church cannot be stated any clearer than that. "The greatest preacher in the world cannot light a fire under a community simply by the force of words."[13] In 1972, James Glasse was president of Lancaster Theological Seminary in Millersville, Pennsylvania. He wrote three words that I never forgot. He actually wrote a book, but I don't remember anything else about the book, just the three words. These words have served me well in all my forty years of ministry and in every different ministry environment: city, town,

---

[12] Jeffrey E. Garten, *The Mind of the C.E.O.*, (Basic Books, New York, 2001), p. 133.

[13] George Barna, *Turn-Around Churches: How to Overcome Barriers to Growth and Bring New Life to an Established Church,* (Regal Books, Ventura, CA, 1993), p. 59.

and suburbia. The three words are "pay the rent."[14] They make ultimate sense to me. It is a formula for disaster when a minister goes into a church and immediately turns everything upside down and inside out and then stirs it all around. But if a minister begins a new ministry and first pays the rent, does all the little things that establish trust, relationship and goodwill, then changes, additions, adaptations, expanding the use of the arts, and welcoming all people are possible. The warm fuzzy stuff can do us in if adequate attention is not given to paying the rent. "In places where a high level of trust has been developed, remarkable change can be accomplished with a minimum of acrimony and delay."[15] Weems uses the letters MBWA to draw attention to a "ministry by wandering around," which is a style of presence required to establish and sustain strong and solid relationships.[16] This is also the focus of MBPTR--"ministry by paying the rent." It was my experience that MBPTR worked: first pay the rent; plenty of goodwill and generosity will often follow.

One of the ways I built a foundation of friendship and trust—paying the rent—was through an intentional ministry of presence. During a twenty-year ministry at Middle Collegiate Church, I never missed a Sunday worship celebration except for the times I was on vacation. Half-an-hour before every celebration my focus was singularly upon greeting, schmoozing, welcoming, hugging, shaking hands, and listening as people arrived. People walked into the sanctuary and there I was with open arms, glad to see them. The children,

---

[14] James D. Glasse, *Putting It Together in the Parish,* (Abingdon Press, Nashville & New York, 1972), p. 53.

[15] Weems, *Take the Next Step,* p. 27.

[16] Weems, *Church Leadership,* p. 53.

youth, and adults could depend upon it. They looked forward to seeing me as they entered church and I looked forward to seeing them coming to church. In the early years when the church was experiencing change, loss, chaos, and the beginnings of new life, the one constant in everybody's church life was that I was there. No matter where I was or what I was doing during the week or even what I was doing earlier that morning, when people arrived for the worship celebration, I was present, focused, and ready to welcome. "Absence does not 'make the heart grow fonder' in congregational life. We come to trust people we know. Building such relationships requires active presence. We know people who are there. Leaders are present and visible."[17] This ministry of presence (MBWA and MBPTR) helped build relationships of trust, friendship, and reliability with both opponents and supporters of the new vision. As the congregation became a new transformed/transforming congregation with a fresh mission and vision, the ministry of presence took on added significance and purpose. The entire new congregation was welcomed, greeted, and loved by me, personally. That made a huge difference in both the internal and external growth of Middle Church.

When we arrived in New York City, one of the first tasks as a family was to enroll our daughter, Cassie, in school. She was entering her junior year in high school. Since it was already July and schools were either filled or didn't accept new students entering in their junior year, our search was hectic and frustrating. We were eventually led to Anne, the admissions director of a school located in the same neighborhood in which we had recently moved. Anne interviewed Cassie

---

[17] Weems, *Taking the Next Step,* p. 29.

and then reported to us what a terrific and talented daughter we had and how delighted she was to welcome Cassie as a student in the fall. From then on, every time we met Anne, she always went out of her way tell us what a delightful person Cassie was and how happy she was to have her as a student. Anne was Cassie's cheerleader. Everybody deserves to have a personal cheerleader who encourages, inspires, acknowledges, and celebrates. Every congregation deserves to have a personal cheerleader. This is what a transformational leader does: encourages, celebrates, acknowledges, and inspires every small step along the journey from death and stagnation to new life. Even when the journey gets tough, especially when the journey gets tough, people and congregations need a personal cheerleader to help keep the journey focused and moving forward. It is what transformational leaders do best.

It is unfortunate that far too many clergy and church leaders do not understand the importance of this simple formula and, therefore, do not give the time and attention paying the rent requires. Relating to people is central to leading and to staying alive during periods of change and transformation. A positive, encouraging attitude is important. My advice when talking to seminarians and young clergy is, if you don't like to relate to a variety of people and if paying the rent is a burden to you or a low priority in your ministry, then move on to another career now. It's not going to work out for you or the church.

People often asked me how was it possible to use all the arts in worship, welcome all of God's diverse rainbow of peoples, and effect all the changes without creating chaos? The answer is simple. First give attention to paying the rent. Then continue paying the rent, all the while constantly dangling the other foot over the edge.

Before starting at Middle I was warned about an elderly person, Alice, who would certainly be an opponent when suggesting changes to the life and worship of the church, even though there were only about twenty-seven active people and, on one Sunday, only eight at worship. After being at Middle for just a short time, I was walking through the social hall when I heard a loud thump of a cane on the floor and a loud voice demanding, "Reverend Dragt, come here." I turned around to see who it was. It was Alice. I walked over to her, placed my arms on her shoulder, put my face directly in front of hers, looked her straight in the eyes and said, "Yes, Alice, what is it?" She looked at my arm resting on her shoulder and answered, "Reverend, flattery will get you nowhere with me." I continued to look into her eyes and replied, "Alice, I have been here for only a few weeks, and I already know that flattery will get me everywhere with you." Alice and I became friends and she became a critical supporter of efforts to reinvent her church. She may have been in her mid-eighties, but when Alice supported something, nobody wanted to mess with her! The art of schmoozing, accepting, building trust, embracing, and welcoming—in other words, MBPTR—is an important first step toward congregational change and transformation.

Sometimes transformational, adaptive leaders may face paying the rent with a very difficult person in extremely unusual, complex, and potentially dangerous circumstances. "Dear Wacko – Be aware. Watch out. I know the way you walk to church in the mornings. You will get what you deserve. This will be your last day." "Dear Wacko – I know you are a phony minister. Say goodbye now. You will not have another chance." Every week for several months, two or three cards with similar messages appeared in the mail. And every week we received two or three phone messages at about five in the morning warning me that this might be my last day alive. Each day I walked different streets to the church, just in case the person was serious about his threats. The newspapers and local TV news are full of stories about people being injured or dying because they didn't take these kinds of threats seriously. The distraught person was an elderly member of the congregation who, before I arrived, was a strong financial contributor and who I was told had a history of unusual behavior and hospitalizations.

It wasn't until later that I became aware of what was making this person so hostile toward me. Three rooms in the church house contained broken and unsafe furniture. One of the rooms in the basement was literally filled with old, discarded items. In a first attempt to begin cleaning the place, a dumpster was rented and filled with all the junk and broken furniture. However, one person's junk may be another person's treasure. All these broken and worn out items were daily picked up from discarded furniture on the street and left on Middle's stoop as gifts by one of its members. When he saw these unappreciated gifts in the dumpster, he snapped. He purchased a gun and ammunition, wrote and mailed threatening cards, left death threats on our home answering machine, and finally the police arrested him waiting for me with a loaded gun in a stairwell across the street from the church house entrance.

The church board invited a psychologist to lead a meeting with his spouse. His spouse never showed up, but at the meeting we came to an understanding about clearing the church house of all the discarded furniture, asking his spouse to take the gun from her husband, and exploring a way to honor him for his long-time support and many previous financial gifts to the church. The church board did not press charges, he was released, we provided a social worker and paid for additional helpful professionals to care for the couple, and made unsuccessful attempts to maintain their regular relationship with the church.

Later, when the person died, I was asked to plan the funeral and to give a eulogy. On my way to the front of the funeral home to begin the ceremony, his spouse grabbed my arm and whispered: "You won't say any of the bad things about him, will you?" I assured her I would never do that and thanked her for asking me to participate in her husband's funeral. "Leadership on the Line: Staying Alive through the Dangers of Leading" is the way Heifetz and Linsky express it. I call it ministry by paying the rent (MBPTR), so we can move forward again toward a new vision for a transformed church. The greatest obstacles to church transformation and to the internal and external growth of a congregation are unnecessary distractions and aimless detours. They can drain a church spiritually and blind a church to its vision. Some of these obstacles, distractions, and detours can be overcome by taking the time to build and maintain relationships with both opponents and supporters.

My advice to leaders is, before anything and everything, first pay the rent. You will be surprised at how many different doors of opportunity paying the rent will open. Nowhere will this be more obvious than in transforming a church's worship from a service to a celebration.

Chapter Ten

Worship as Celebration
One foot planted in the center, the other dangling off the edge

We moved to New York City from Chapel Hill, North Carolina, and lived in Stuyvesant Town at 14th Street and Avenue B, a housing development that had more residents than the entire town of Chapel Hill. The main subway line for us was the L-train. My experience was similar to one I once read in a book I can no longer recall. One day I went into the nearest station and sat on a bench to wait for the train. There were only four of us—all sitting next to each other; two with eyes closed; all four with legs crossed; two staring forward with blank expressions on our faces. There we sat; silent, almost lifeless, like one of those stone sculptures you sometimes see in city parks or on college campuses. All of a sudden we were startled when someone stumbled down the stairs, leaned against a metal post, laughing hysterically, and screaming at the top of his voice: "Hey, what is it with this place? It's like a church down here!" Just then, the subway came; the four of us quickly got on and left the person precariously holding onto the post, still laughing.

One of the constants in my ministry is an untiring, intentional quest to rescue the church's worship from being too boring and too irrelevant, but at the same time, to remain connected to the church's rich history and traditions. It is important when planning the church's worship to have one foot planted in the center while dangling the other off the edge. Middle Collegiate Church has been in the city since 1729 with Collegiate roots going back to 1628. You can't get much more solidly planted than that (one foot planted in the center). Yet Middle constantly pushed the boundaries of what church and worship can be (the other foot dangling off the edge).

I called what happens on Sunday mornings a worship celebration. To understand worship as celebration is critical not only to resurrecting a dead church back to life, but is also important for the use of the arts in worship and for opening doors for multicultural and multiracial participation.

The idea of worship as celebration is nothing new, of course. It is as old as the Bible itself. Considering the broad scope of the biblical message, the older testament is dominated by the Exodus event, the newer testament by Easter. They both represent the hope of dramatic new life possibilities for individuals and for humankind. They both are highly festive, arts expressive, and celebrative events. And they both determine the focus and the character of public worship, instead of modeling Sunday worship after our private or personal devotional and meditation practices. It is by design, not by accident, that the church gathers on Sundays for worship, because historically Sunday is intended to be a weekly celebration of Easter. Sunday is a time when we publicly gather to celebrate the whole of life—life in all of its possibilities and hope; in all of its frustrations and disappointments; in all of its dedication to justice, peace on earth, and good will to all. When we walk through the doors of the church on Sunday mornings, the greetings we receive, the music we hear, the sanctuary environment we enter, and the anticipation we feel inside us should all resurrect our spirits, heighten our anticipation, and raise our person to a higher level of spirituality and, therefore, to a higher level of human existence. Sundays are little Easters. The jazz musician John Coltrain said, "Good worship, like good jazz, should uplift and inspire us to reach greater capacities for a more meaningful life." When that happens for us on Sunday mornings, we have experienced worship as celebration. That is also where the first signs of congregational transformation will appear. Bringing a stagnant, dysfunctional, declining, or dying church back to life begins with vision, which first takes shape in the transformation of the Sunday worship from a service to a celebration.

In my entire forty years in the ministry, I have intentionally never, ever used the words "worship service" to refer to what we do on Sunday mornings. The term irritates my ears. The words don't say it for me. To me, they imply worship more out of duty than out of joy; worship more out of ritual than expressed by the arts; more out of talking about God and human community instead of experiencing God and human community; worship more out of obligation instead of gratitude; more out of set patterns, traditions, and routine liturgies instead of allowing the Spirit to guide us. To me the words "worship service" imply doing what we've always been doing and, of course, that often means we will keep getting what we've always been getting. The arts-expressive celebration of Exodus and Easter is missing from the term "worship service." If someone asked, "Gordon, do you want to go with

79

me on Sunday morning to a worship service or to a worship celebration?" I would always choose the celebration.

Worship celebration affirms diversity in the planning of the total worship experience. Celebrating worship includes diverse traditions, music, instruments, singing, dance, theater, preaching, and personal expressions of response. That is the really big difference between a worship service and a worship celebration.

I confess there were a few moments when I did let my passion for Sunday celebration and diversity lead me to do some dumb things. These are the times when I temporarily forgot to always have one foot planted solidly in the center while dangling the other over the edge. It doesn't work to plant both feet deeply in the center, nor does it work to dangle both feet over the edge. The one can cause complete immobility and stagnation, while the other can cause imbalance and a crash. Both have ego issues. This is what happened on a Sunday when I planned to ride a small foot-propelled scooter alongside Middle's float in New York City's annual Pride Day Parade down Fifth Avenue. I brought the scooter with me to church so I could join the parade immediately following worship. The closer it got to the time when the worship was to begin, I thought it would be great fun to ride the scooter into the sanctuary as a sort of surprise, festive processional. I went to the social hall, picked up the scooter, and when the congregation began singing the opening hymn, wearing my usual bright red clergy robe, I got on the scooter and excitingly pushed it down the center aisle. By the time I got up front, I was a little out of control (literally, spiritually, and figuratively). I made a sharp turn to avoid the communion table, the small front wheel of the scooter got caught in the carpet, and I went headfirst over the handlebars, only narrowly avoiding crashing into the choir loft. Lying on the floor, I thought, "God, I guess you didn't think this was such a good idea, did you?" Embarrassingly, I picked myself up. The congregation was singing the final words to the opening hymn: "Glory, glory hallelujah, since I laid my burdens down." When I faced the congregation, they responded with a thunderous applause and were all relieved that both the hymn and my fall ended well. Sunday morning is a worship celebration with one foot planted in the center, while the other foot dangles over the edge.

I may have always used the term "worship celebration" instead of "worship service," but I have not always been successful in encouraging others to do the same. For as long as I can remember, I've printed the words "worship celebration" in articles, spoken them at workshops and conferences, posted them on bulletin boards in front of the church, taught them in classes at Middle and at conferences, preached them from the pulpit, and modeled them in worship every Sunday. I sometimes feel, however, it has been one of the greatest failures of communication in my ministry. The term "worship service" is so entrenched in our congregations and in society that very few people from any of the congregations I served ever consistently picked up on what to me is a fundamental idea. When Anna, who had been an associate at Middle, moved to a church in Queens, I called her and got the church's answering machine. I heard Anna's voice say: "Welcome, our Sunday worship celebration is at …" I was startled. I hung up, leaned back, and laughed. Finally, finally, after so many years in the ministry and so much intentional educational effort, one other person got it. She also posted "worship celebration" on the bulletin board outside the church. My ministry was successful after all. Since then, a few other colleagues and parishioners have been heard using the term, but certainly that is not much accomplishment after making it a priority in ministry for over forty years. "Not that I have already obtained this or have already reached the goal, but I nevertheless press on," says the Apostle Paul ... and me.

An important characteristic of a worship celebration is quality. Quality inspires and attracts. Quality is intentional, planned, and involves team work. Quality is never a result of winging it.

Chapter Eleven

Never Wing It
Nurture the passion

The quality of the Sunday morning worship celebration is critical to bringing a dead church back to life. I cannot imagine the call to ministry means doing anything other than the very best we can on any given Sunday. Think about how many options people have on Sunday mornings. God causes a stir or restlessness or speaks a quiet inner message with people to encourage or nudge them to make the choice of going to a worship celebration. It is up to the ministers and worship leaders to joyfully welcome, accept, embrace, be prepared, and do the very best we can every Sunday. Depending upon our current physical, spiritual, and personal circumstances, we may be able to do better on one Sunday than on another, but no matter what, it is a responsibility of our calling to be prepared and to do the very best we can at any given time.

I did not have the gifts to be a great preacher. But that was no excuse to not be as prepared and as good as I could possibly be. It is okay to be a good enough preacher.[18] I worked hard at preaching. During the week, I reflected on the sermon on several occasions and often wrote it out on Friday mornings. I got back at it again early Saturday mornings, sitting by myself in the sanctuary, rehearsing my sermon over and over and over; editing, editing and editing it some more; cutting, cutting and cutting it until the sermon was concise and approximately fifteen minutes long. When I felt it was a sermon and was the very best I could do at that moment, I put my notebook away, repeated "thanks be to God" several times, shut off the lights, closed the doors, and went home to watch a basketball game. I went through the same process early Sunday morning. Some of us have to work harder at preaching than others. All of us are called to do our best. Our call demands it. There is no place in the ministry for winging it. I have little empathy for clergy who claim to be so busy that they end up writing their sermons on Saturday nights or Sunday mornings, and that's what their preaching often sounds like, too. Winging it can become habit-forming, and it is the congregation that suffers.

But why suggest a concise twelve-to-fifteen minute sermon? I have been asked that question so many times, especially by other clergy, most of who disagree with me. There are some clergy today who feel sermons need to be approximately thirty minutes long. Better them than me, and better their congregations than Middle Church. I didn't want the sermon to dominate worship like that, and if I was a participant in worship, I for sure didn't want to listen to a sermon

---

[18] To explore the concept of "good enough," see D.W. Winnicott, *Home is Where We Start From: Essays by a Psychoanalyst* (W.W. Norton & Company, 1986).

that long, no matter how good it was. There is nothing magic or absolute about a twelve-to-fifteen minute target; it is, instead, a guideline to remind us that more is not always better, longer is not always superior, and there are a lot of other elements in the worship celebration to be considered.

The time is long overdue for clergy to realize there are other ways than preaching a sermon to communicate the Gospel, worship God, and nurture each other in the faith. I was committed to preaching and doing the best I could, but I was equally committed to using the arts in worship. Nonverbal, visual, and musical communications are as important, powerful, biblical, and nurturing as the verbal. There is no reason for one form of communication to dominate another and, quite simply, if we can't say it in twelve or fifteen minutes, fifteen more isn't going to help. Maybe one of the problems is that it takes much more work to prepare, develop, and deliver a fifteen minute sermon that says something than it does to write and deliver a thirty minute sermon that wanders all over the biblical and theological terrain. It also takes a lot more work to plan and develop a total worship celebration which includes both the verbal and a variety of the arts. Worship as celebration places more emphasis upon experiencing God than upon talking about God. The second verse of Jane Parker Huber's song "God of Wisdom, Truth, and Beauty" is a good guiding song for planning a worship celebration:

God of drama, music, dancing, God of story, sculpture, art,
God of wit, all life enhancing, God of every yearning heart:
Challenge us with quests of spirit, Truth revealed in myriad ways,

Word or song for hearts that hear it, sketch and
model--forms of praise.[19]

A member of the church died from complications from
HIV/AIDS. He was thirty-seven years old and recently pro-
moted to an executive position in the company in which he
worked. Every Sunday for months we witnessed his body
wasting away until he became more spirit than body. When
he died, a memorial was held celebrating his person and life.
Words were not enough to express his belief in a God who,
at his death, would embrace his spirit and lift it into God's
presence. Dancers were asked to choreograph this person's
faith and what some of the congregation might be feeling
during the memorial. Before the choreographer began to put
her ideas into form, she talked with members of the deceased
person's family and friends and with members of the congregation. She chose the dancers and then had several planning
sessions to get their input into the choreography. Finally, they
scheduled three rehearsals. All of this planning and rehearsing
took place in a very short period of time. The worship began
with spoken words. Then the dancers came down the aisles
of the church in movements that expressed a loving and understanding God and a mourning and thankful congregation.
The dancers embraced the urn containing the person's ashes,
lifted up the urn above their heads, carried it in the midst of
the congregation, and then out of the church. The silence in
the sanctuary was interrupted only by the sounds of people
crying—then by applause, followed by a standing ovation,
and finally conversation, hugging, stories, and laughter filled

---

[19] From *A Singing Faith* by Jane Parker Huber. © 1981 Jane Parker
Huber. Used by permission of Westminister John Knox Press.

the sanctuary. It was a worship celebration filled with experience more than talk.

To include the arts in a worship celebration doesn't mean that they, too, cannot suffer from a practice of winging it. I've seen it often. Dance, theater, pageants, puppets, props, sound considerations, choirs, soloists, instrumentalists, and bands all need time for planning, rehearsing, and understanding their proper placement within the flow and theme of the worship. When children are used, special attention needs to be given so they become an essential part of the total and not just added props to look cute while others perform the real and important parts. Worship planning is the key; otherwise, there are too many opportunities for winging it. No congregation deserves that. No minister's call into the ministry can endure that. There is no hope of bringing a dysfunctional or dead church back to life by winging it, and there is no greater partner in resurrecting a stagnant or dying congregation than a quality worship celebration. The reverse is also true. There is no greater contributor to a stagnant or dying congregation than a worship celebration and/or sermon put together by last minute planning and inadequate preparation.

One of the best antidotes to winging it is to nurture a passion for ministry, for life, and for people. I find it to be generally true, that if you show me a person who does ministry with a passion, I'll show you a person who isn't apathetic and doesn't short circuit appropriate preparation; I'll also show you a congregation that is on the way toward transformation and new life. Passion in the ministry is intentional, transformative, adaptive leadership; it is leadership Spirit-filled; it is movement with intent and vision from the action to reflection to adaptation and back to action again. When I hear church leaders being rigid, worried over who is in and who is out, intense over correct interpretations, doctrine, and practices, and inflexible in worship planning, I ask myself, "Man, woman, where is your passion?" A dead church will only be raised to new life by church leaders who nurture passion within themselves and who model a passion for ministry, life, and people.

A person who leads with passion is less likely to wing it in the ministry and more likely to be creative, innovative, prepared, and concerned about always presenting the very best one can for the people of the congregation and the community. A person who approaches ministry with a passion for life and for people is also more likely to listen, respond, and adapt, instead of demanding that everything be done "correctly" and in strict compliance with denominational policy, established rules, traditions, and rituals. There are church leaders who jump from one extreme to another—they either make leading so simple that action without necessary planning and vision becomes a way of their professional lives, or they make it so complex that there is no wiggle room in their belief and practice. "I am about to do a new thing; now it springs forth, do you not perceive it?" (Isaiah 43:19a). "We need a renewal of passion in ministry. We need a ministry characterized by a passion that can only come from a compelling message and an essential vision. People will always be weary of cures that don't cure, blessings that don't bless, and solutions that don't solve. This is a great moment for a passionate ministry."[20]

I grew up in an environment in which emotions and passion were publicly controlled and rarely expressed. Early in my ministry I sometimes worried about how emotionally and

---

[20] Weems, *Church Leadership,* p. 135.

passionately I felt about circumstances and people. On one occasion, I was sharing with a congregation something about which I felt deeply when tears began to well up from inside me. Just then I overheard our daughter, who was sitting in the front row with a friend, say, "Don't worry about my dad, that's just who he is." That's who I am—an emotional, passionate, and compassionate person. I felt an incredible relief. What a moment. I received permission from my daughter to be who I am. I never again worried about being emotional and passionate.

I was initially introduced to passion in life and ministry when I graduated from seminary, moved half-way across the country to accept my first call, and met Gene, the minister in a nearby church. He had recently seen the movie *Zorba the Greek* and was spiritually and personally overwhelmed by the experience. The movie renewed in him an intense passion for life and for the church's ministry. He called it being filled with "the Zorbic"—loving life, loving people, dancing exuberantly the dance of life, and living life to the fullest. For him, Zorba was the Christ-figure; to be filled with the Zorbic was being filled with the Spirit. Gene had an incredible and lasting impact upon my life and the focus of my ministry. Growing up in a small, rural Midwest community, I had never seen anything like it before, never felt anything like it before, and never envisioned ministry like it before. Passion and ministry are inseparable. I cannot imagine bringing a stagnant or dying church back to life without passion.

When Jesus was in a rather socially complex and politically charged environment, he was asked to describe his faith. Jesus said, "I have come to be with you, that you may have life, and that you may have life, abundantly." That's it. That's all. What is important is for church leaders to have a passion for ministry, for life, and for people. That's it. That's all. There is no place in the ministry for slackers who simply go from week-to-week doing more of the same and getting more of the same results.

I was once invited to participate in a denominationally sponsored diversity retreat. At the beginning of the retreat, to get us all more acquainted with one another and more relaxed in our strange environment, we played a fun word game. The leader announced a word or a phrase, then the opposite of that word or phrase. If we believed or identified with the first phrase, we sat on one side of the room. If we believed or identified more with the opposite, we moved our chairs to the other side of the room: "Are you liberal or conservative? Are you evangelical or mainline?" and so on. One choice that generated some excitement was: "Are you more infra-lapsarian or supra-lapsarian?" At that point, I said to myself, "Huh?" Everybody else in the room seemed to know exactly where they stood. But I didn't have a clue and I was positive infra-lapsarian and supra-lapsarian wouldn't play well on the streets of the East Village in New York City. So I put my chair in the middle of the room and sat there by myself. Then the leader said, "Are you more orthodox or more heretic?" Ah, finally, I knew exactly where I was on that one.

After the game, I thought, there are too many big words in the church's liturgy and vocabulary that are irrelevant to the person on the street. There is too much stuff in the church's life and worship that doesn't make one bit of differ-ence in resurrecting a stagnant, declining church. There is too much in the ministry that can easily lead one to winging it. What is really needed is a fundamental passion for ministry. What is really needed is a passion to help people and churches live life to the fullest. "Grant us wisdom, grant us courage, for the living of these days, for the living of these days," is the way Harry Emerson Fosdick expressed it in the hymn, "God of Grace and God of Glory."

I get a similar inspiration from an early silent movie performer, director, and composer, Charlie Chaplin. His tramp character captures my attention most. "I am always aware that Charlie is playing with death. He plays with it, mocks it, thumbs his nose at it, but never, ever gets use to it. He is always terribly aware of being alive at every moment."[21] That, says Chaplin, is the only purpose of the tramp character—to bring more life to himself and to others. That is the best we can do and is the essence of passion for church leaders—to always be terribly aware of being alive and to try the very best we can to bring more life into wherever we are and into whatever we do.

I have come, says Jesus, and so have we church leaders come, to be with people, the community, and the church, that we all may have life, and that we all may have life, abundantly. Nurture the passion.

Leading with passion, confident of being called, and dedicated to bringing life and life abundantly into our ministry and worship are all qualities supported and encouraged by the use of the arts in the life, worship, and ministry of the church. We welcome and celebrate the arts because it's biblical and the arts work.

---

[21] Robert Payne, *The Great God Plan,* (Hermitage House, New York, 1952), p.20.

91

Chapter Twelve

The Arts in the Worship
and Life of the Church
Because it's biblical, and it works

I based the use of the arts in Middle's worship and life upon four fundamental principles. First, the Easter principle. Sunday worship celebration is intended by design, not by accident, to be a weekly festive, creative, visual Easter celebration for the purpose of raising up people's spirits, lives, and commitments. Even the forty days of Lent do not include the Sundays. Every person and church needs festive, Easter experiences.

Second, the biblical principle. The two senior citizens, Sarah and Abraham, are models of responding to God's call to live a life of continuously breaking out of old forms and patterns and moving outward by faith toward new structures and practices. Miriam is the first recorded celebration dancer in the Bible. David is a poet, songwriter, singer, and dancer. And who can imagine celebrating Advent/Christmas without the arts? There is also the Apostle Paul's terrific imagery of the body of Christ with all the diverse parts, persons, gifts, and talents important to the functioning of the whole. The creation story is filled with variety, diversity, and the arts, which open new doors and create new entry points. Opening more doors and creating more entry points are fundamental to the resurrection of a stagnant, declining, or dying church.

Third, the boredom principle. When I was young, I used to sit in church on Sunday mornings and count the number of tile squares in the ceiling. As an adult I am still often bored, but now by the use of so many irrelevant words, phrases, and actions in liturgies and ceremonies. United Methodist Bishop William Willimon, in a sermon at the Duke University Chapel, pointed out what sometimes happens to people when they walk into a church: "It doesn't make sense," he said. "Perfectly happy and energetic folks become quiet, somber and motionless. Accepting, welcoming, and generous folks become conservative, critical, excluding, and intolerant. No wonder God said, 'I hate your pious religious assemblies. I cannot stand them.'" This is why I call what happens on Sunday mornings a worship celebration, not a worship service. Boredom on Sunday mornings is not passable or acceptable. It is not good enough for a church to plan its worship celebrations in less than the most dynamic ways possible. It is not satisfactory for the church to use anything but the best tools for celebration, worship, and ministry, and the most creative energies and skills with which to carry out its vision and mission. "What time is it?" "Whose time is it?" It is time for the church to use in its worship and ministry joy, dance, poetry, a diversity of music and expression, and the fullness of God's Spirit of creativity.

We need jugglers and high-wire artists —

sequined, sparkling and dancing on the void –
if theology is to measure up at all to the magnificent God whose gambling habits and
sleights of hand boggle our simple minds. We
need a deeply imaginative meditation on the
narratives and symbols of our past if we hope
to co-create a future. We need a powerful vision of the beauty of God and the beauty of
her creation … [We need] those who will ride
the wild storm cloud and hide in the clefts of
the rock just to see the hinder parts of God.
We won't get any of this until the poets are
embraced and allowed, encouraged, and loved
into running all the risks they want.[22]

Such creativity can only happen if growth and transformation are essential ingredients of a church's vision. The use
of the arts in worship is a remedy for boredom and irrele-
vancy. There has never been a better time than now for the
use of the arts in the worship, life, and ministry of the church.

Fourth, the practical principle. The arts work. I have been
a minister in a variety of churches and settings. In all the different situations and environments, inclusion of the arts
brought new energy, life, diversity, and extraordinary spiritual
and numerical growth. The easiest first step is with the music.
Present a variety of music to represent the diversity of God's
beautiful multicultural creation. Add instruments. Include a
band, orchestra, or quartet representing a variety of different
musical traditions. Middle occasionally used steel drummers

---

[22] Sara Maitland, *A Big-Enough God: A Feminist's Search for a Joyful Theology,* (Henry Holt and Company, New York, 1995), p. 145.

and even a full steel drum orchestra. A traditional choir, gospel choir, and jazz band regularly performed in the worship. Sing hymns and anthems that can include a variety of people and are not just by white European composers who died four hundred years ago. Take care, however, that some of the old favorites and great music of the past remain a part of the repertoire. Create a diverse gospel choir and band. Few things produce more new entry points and open more new doors into a church than an active, vital, and multicultural gospel choir. Ask a dancer to dance a prayer, accompanied by a piano or drum or stringed instrument or saxophone. Invite a group of dancers to dance the theme of the sermon, a biblical text, or the liturgical season.

On one occasion, I read the Pentecost story while a dancer danced it, energetically snapping a fifteen-foot red ribbon above the heads of the congregation. It was one thing to listen to a story about the wind and the tongues of fire; it was quite another thing to actually experience the wind and the tongues of fire right above our very own heads. On another occasion, the Palm Sunday story was read while dancers danced the story. Seventeen large, twelve-foot puppets were the crowd, the gospel choir sang, and two people dressed in a donkey costume danced "with Jesus" into the church down the center aisle. The story ended with the gospel choir leading the entire congregation in singing and dancing "The Lord of the Dance" while palms were distributed to everyone. The performance filled the sanctuary with terrific energy, participation, and spirit. Include a jazz band that can play authentic jazz arrangements of familiar hymns, songs, and spirituals for half an hour while people are gathering before the worship celebration. On occasion, the jazz band at Middle was placed outside on the sidewalk near the main entrance of the church.

Not just churchgoers would stop on Second Avenue to listen before entering the church but also passersby and people in taxis, cars, and trucks. Others waved or blew their horns as they passed the church. The music created an uplifting, happy environment in the community and through which people entered into the church.

Some jazz bands, however, can be too "churchy" when they play in a church on Sunday mornings. Be careful about that, especially if you are interested in adding something new instead of simply doing a different variation of the same old thing. Make sure the jazz band is capable of playing church songs "jazzy." A long and creative partnership was established with a jazz group at Middle Collegiate Church, but the association had a shaky start. Before the group played, they were given a list of familiar hymns, songs, and spirituals, and encouraged to add some of their own. Then I talked with them about my expectations of not wanting the selections played in a traditional church style, but as authentic jazz pieces. They were asked to play in church like they played in a bar or a gig on Saturday nights. Sunday morning came and the first song played by these professional jazz musicians was a familiar hymn that sounded like it was being performed by an amateur Sunday school band trying to play an unfamiliar hymn in a stereotypical church fashion. It was so embarrassing that I asked the pianist and director to end the piece and go on to something else. It is difficult to overcome the many stereotypes a great number of people have about church and the Sunday morning worship time. Following the celebration, I told the group this would be the first and last time they would appear at Middle if they could not figure out how to perform these songs like they were performing in a bar, not in a church. They changed and authentic jazz became a great

addition to the worship celebrations and a popular entry
point for new and more diverse people to come into the
church. The arts work.

I am very skeptical about using the terms "sacred dance"
or "liturgical dance." When I see these terms, I automatically
ask the question, "What's that?" "To call one segment of any
art form sacred implies that the rest of that form is unac-
ceptably secular and suspect."[23] The terms "sacred dance"
and "liturgical dance" communicate the wrong message. I
have seen too many dances in worship referred to as "liturgical dance" that have been no more than jumping around and
waving arms for Jesus. When I include dance in a worship
celebration, I want the choreographer and some of the participants to be trained and experienced dancers. Others from
the congregation may be included in the mix, but this gives
the performance a sense of integrity, authenticity, and quality
as dance.

There was one occasion when I asked a dancer to choreograph a four-week series for the Advent/Christmas season. She said "I would love to, but what is Advent?" She was
unfamiliar with the traditional church language. I know some
church leaders who would have immediately eliminated her
from consideration. I quickly accepted her offer. She was a
trained and experienced choreographer and dancer who, I
was convinced, would approach the Advent/Christmas season completely fresh. It was exactly what I was looking for. I
was excited about the possibility. Here was a person who
would not be encumbered by traditional interpretations of

---

[23] Judith Rock, *Performer as Priest & Prophet: Restoring the Intuitive in Worship Through Music & Dance,* (Harper & Row, Publishers, San Francisco,
1988), p. 35.

this very familiar story. Here was a person who could think new thoughts and explore new approaches to a story that for many of us had become too familiar to risk going beyond the way we have always thought of it. I could not wait for her to get started. She created a terrific, spiritually uplifting Advent/Christmas series using trained and experienced dancers, along with other adults and children from the congregation.

Over the next few years I asked her to create new pieces for this same important season in the church year. But before confirming her return, each time I asked if she could still be new and creative or was Middle's space and the Advent/Christmas story now too familiar for her to still be challenging and fresh? That was the approach I took with all persons asked to be leaders in Middle's worship celebrations, including clergy and lay, professionals and volunteers. That is a question I constantly asked myself, too. After planning twenty-nine Advent/Christmas seasons, was I still capable of being fresh to plan a thirtieth? Did I still hear God speaking through the story, and could I still be innovative and creative in the space that had become so familiar to me? It is too easy in these important celebrations in the worship life of the church to rely upon traditional resources or to simply tweak the same things we have always been doing. We convince ourselves we are too busy to be fresh and creative, which is a sure formula for a church to become stagnant and declining.

It is important for transformational leaders to build and maintain a positive network of artistic people upon which one can depend when planning worship celebrations and other events. In the late sixties, I was the coordinating minister of a new church start which met in a renovated barn located in the middle of a suburban housing development. One of the most unusual decisions of my entire forty years of ministry was to hire a seventh grader as the music director of the church. I first noticed him when he was featured in many local school, theater, and concert productions. He was talented, popular, and acted like a seventh grader. Every Sunday morning, Doug and I invited area musicians to join him to form a band which performed for that Sunday morning's worship celebration. Doug had the ability to quickly write charts for and include a diverse group of musicians and instruments into an incredibly eclectic and exciting band. Dancers, choreographers, singers, composers, poets, writers, and actors were attracted to the church, mainly because of the music and the inclusion of the arts in the church's worship and ministry. The collaboration and friendship with this young, talented music director established the new church as a regional center for the arts in worship. The church experienced a rapid growth, especially among the area's youth. The performing arts worked. Doug later moved to New York City and began a successful career composing and directing on Broadway and Off-Broadway and creating a host of popular advertising jingles. Because of his unique gifts for arranging music and improvising during performances, I invited him to Middle on several occasions as a guest accompanist for special dance productions and for performances of the Jerriese Johnson East Village Gospel Choir. At a couple of his performances at Middle, I scheduled the spiritual "The Lord of the Dance." No one could play the song with the spirit and the energy he put into it. He had the ability to raise the level of joy and participation in the sanctuary to the point where people would literally dance "The Lord of the Dance" in the pews and aisles.

At another time when I celebrated my fiftieth birthday, Doug was invited to compose and perform a song about our early relationship and experiences in worship and the arts.

Before he sang, he told the gathering at Middle Collegiate Church, "Can you figure Gordon out? People say he's a leader in using the arts in the worship and life of the church. A leader in using the arts? Why, he can't keep a beat. When the gospel choir is singing and the congregation is clapping their hands to the beat of the music, watch Gordon. He's either off beat or is visibly following someone in the choir or the congregation. He can't sing. Have you ever heard him during the singing of a hymn when he forgets to turn off his mic? The tech person at the back of the church is wildly waving his hands to tell him to turn it off. A Middle Church choir member once gave him a tongue-in-cheek compliment, when he said 'Gordon sings off tune, but the good thing is that he is consistently off tune.' He can't dance. I know you've seen him dance here on some Sunday mornings, but it's quite a sight. I'm surprised he's willing to be persuaded by a choreographer to embarrass himself like that in front of the congregation. He can't play an instrument. He can't act. He can't draw or paint or take interesting photos. Come to think of it, when it comes to the arts, he doesn't seem to be able to do anything well by himself, but he always has all these creative arts people around him. What's that about? Whenever and wherever I see him, there he is surrounded by singers, musicians, writers, actors, poets, fine artists, photographers, choreographers, dancers, and skilled preachers. That's pretty great. That's the thing he does really well."

I cannot remember anyone ever critiquing my weaknesses and defining my strengths quite that bluntly. Doug was right. He put his finger on exactly what I did best. Apart from delivering a sermon on Sunday mornings, not many church leaders are talented in the performing and fine arts. Maybe seminary training should require instruction in dancing, acting, singing, painting, and art history. It can, however, be a benefit for church leaders unskilled in the arts to employ the arts in worship and ministry. It is important to be aware of our limitations and to develop the appropriate skills to bring others into leadership roles who are experts in the many areas of the arts in which we are not. Transformational leaders know how to recognize, celebrate, challenge, and include the gifts of the artists without getting their own egos in the way of the integrity of the artists to express their own gifts. The artists know best how to do what they do. As church leaders, we need to do what we do best—to draw artists into the worship and life of the church and to produce an arts-friendly worship and ministry. That is a key leadership quality which will serve a transformational ministry well. I cannot imagine resurrecting a stagnant and declining church without the arts.

Doug later sang his birthday tribute, "Standing the Test of Time," which is also a testimony to a long twenty-year relationship of two persons, first as colleagues and later as enduring friends:

> There we were; making a difference
> Sending a message; getting things done
> Here we are; we are a part of our future
> You are still the father; now I've got a son
> And time, time just disappears
> Suddenly with years; all begins to mingle
> And I'm better for those years and memories
> All fit together; always a part of time.
> Look at us; everything is nifty
> I am playing music; you are chatting with the
>   Lord
> Could it be you are turning fifty

Twenty-odd years now since we've been accord
While time, time just tries to seal
All the things we feel
Making us who we were
We climb up to see what is real
And always you are here inside me
Standing the test of time.
Days come and decades go
Who can tell why or how
We barely talk, but what do you know
I loved you then and I love you now
And time, time just slips away faster every day
Telling us that life can be so sublime
This I have to say, that I will always remember
Who you are and what you do
While I have you and time.

The congregation appreciated the candor and humor of his speech. As an outsider to Middle, Doug said things members of the congregation had noticed and thought but didn't dare say. Following the singing of the song, some were affected emotionally and spiritually by the obvious love, respect, and friendship which had endured time and distance over many years between two former colleagues. For all present that day, Doug raised the level of the relationship that can exist between members of a church staff. It is frequently true that the best quality and most creative worship celebrations and programs are the results of a relationship between the church staff, volunteers, and artists in which the presence of love, respect, and friendship are greater than the existence of tension, miscommunication, and conflict.

Two very familiar biblical stories provided much of my

inspiration for using the arts in the worship of the church: the creation story in Genesis and the Christmas story in the Gospels. In the creator's eyes, all of creation is good. Life is a gift from God. To be in relationship with and to enjoy the many diverse gifts of creation is to be in relationship with and to enjoy the Giver. To experience the variety and diversity of creation is to experience the variety and diversity of the Creator. The story is about beauty, diversity and fullness, and God says it is all good. God challenges us with a creative spirituality to live by. It is a creative spirituality that embraces creativity, the arts, and celebration. It embraces the justice of welcoming and accepting all people, no matter whom, no matter what, no matter where one is on one's faith or life journey. This amazing story concludes with human beings created in God's diverse image. Incredibly, we are all partners with God in the creative business. Can you believe it? We human beings are partners with God in creativity. We too are gifted with the very same creative spirit as God. A creative spirituality says God didn't finish speaking, creating, loving, accepting, challenging, caring, or celebrating at the end of Genesis Chapter Two or Revelation Chapter Twenty-two. "God is still speaking" is the way the United Church of Christ denomination put it in one of their advertising campaigns. Forget arguments about creationism, intelligent design, and literalism. "God is still speaking." Life is an on-going performing art. It is this creative spirituality of the arts, diversity, and imagination in worship, inspired by the creation story, that helped resurrect Middle Collegiate Church from near death to where it is now, and Middle and we are by no means finished and God is by no means finished with Middle and us.

I recall reading an interview with Leonard Bernstein in which he said music is "cosmos in chaos." That idea stuck in my mind for years because, of course, that is exactly what the creation story is about. It is a movement, a journey, a drama, a dance from chaos (meaningless existence) to cosmos (meaningful existence). And that is also the movement and purpose of the arts in the church.

One of my favorite arts seasons of the church year is the Advent/Christmas season. Advent/Christmas is the embodiment of the arts alive in the church. I cannot imagine celebrating this important and transforming season without the arts. The biblical writers sure didn't. They wrote about angels singing and dancing, trumpets proclaiming, stars shining, candles burning, flowers blooming, anticipation challenging, hope alive, shepherds moving, people journeying, gift giving, animals wondering, and Mary and Joseph giving birth. It is the arts that can really make Advent/Christmas come alive for us in all of the season's beauty, meaning, spirituality and fullness.

It is not a stretch to say that whenever we use the arts in the life, worship and ministry of the church, we are in essence celebrating an important meaning of Advent/Christmas. Advent/Christmas is about the incarnation, birthing, and calling forth the spirit of God in human form. Advent/Christmas focuses upon giving life and creativity. That is what the performing and fine arts do so well.

And the angel said to her, "Don't be afraid, Mary. God has been gracious to you. You will become pregnant and give birth to a son and you will name him Jesus." Mary replied, "That, Gabriel, is impossible." The angel answered, "The Holy Spirit will move within you and God's power will rest upon you." And Mary said what every artist, transformational leader, and birth-giver must eventually say: "Behold, O God, I am your servant. Let it be unto me according to your word."

105

And there we have it. God called Mary to do what in her eyes and in our eyes and the world's eyes is absolutely impossible. It cannot rationally happen. We all know that. But instead of saying, "No, I cannot do it," Mary said, "Yes, God. I will not be afraid to be a birth-giver, to be a creator of something new and fresh, to be an artist, and a transformational leader. Yes, God. Be it unto me according to your word." Yes, God. Call us and call your church to be artists. Yes, God. Call us to do the impossible. Yes, God. Call us to be intentional, transformational, adaptive leaders capable of resurrecting dysfunctional, declining, and dying churches back to incredible new life. Yes, God. Call us to be birth-givers, to bring forth fresh life, a new understanding, a different perspective, an added dimension. Yes, God. Be it unto me, unto us, our church, our nation, and our world according to your word. Advent/Christmas says to make something new and to experience transformation, sometimes the unthinkable, even the impossible, has to be tried. The arts can communicate this message best.

I love the pageantry and symbolism of the Advent wreath. It was always one of my favorite tools for teaching and celebrating. It is filled with great festive, anticipatory, and educational possibilities. Every Advent/Christmas season I created a major production of dance, music, words, and pageantry around lighting the candles of the wreath. As a congregation, we traveled the Advent journey together from one candle to another and finally to the Christ candle. The opportunity for the use of the arts in this special season shouldn't be missed. People expect it; they anticipate it; we are encouraged to deliver it. Advent/Christmas and the arts have terrific possibilities together.

When considering which candles to use on the Advent

wreath, the Christ candle should never be the traditional white, associating the color white with purity, wholeness, and Christ. In multicultural, multiracial environments, green is a much better choice, representing life, growth, possibilities, and evergreen. I also believed purple, which is the color of reflection and examination, was the best color for all four weeks of Advent. This is how I sometimes expressed in words the joy, anticipation, and abundant creative imagery of the Advent/Christmas journey:

> Advent is any time of the week,
> the month, or the year,
> when we intentionally
> do whatever it will take
> for the hope and celebration
> of Christmas to happen
> for us, our city, and our world.
> One of the very special symbols
> of this season is the Advent Wreath.
> The wreath is green; the color of life
> and growth. The wreath is circular;
> representing wholeness, community and
> connected relationships. The wreath contains five
>   candles:
> four candles represent the four weeks before
>   Christmas.
> The purple color of these candles reminds us
> that the four weeks are a time for considering
> decisions, choices, and actions, which will help
> make the birthing of the new life that is Christmas
>   happen
> for us, our city, our nation and world this year and

every year.

The fifth candle is the Christmas Candle. The Christ
Candle.

It is green because it represents life and the possibility for new life.

It represents hope and a future worth living.

It is the candle of blessing.

It stands in the center, proclaiming

"Peace, peace on earth;

goodwill, goodwill to all persons, peoples, and nations

and us this year."

Each week in Advent we light a candle

hoping for Christmas;

praying for Christmas

not to pass us by

this year.

Then the angel of God stood (stands) before them
(us),

And the glory of God shone (shines) around them
(us),

And they (we) were (are) terrified.

But the angel said (says) to them (us),

"Do not be afraid" (do not be afraid, do not be afraid,
live on)

For you see – I am bringing you (us) good news of
great joy

For all the people:

To you (us) is born this day (today, tomorrow, every
day)

In the city of David (New York City, New Jersey,

California)
A Savior, who is the Christ.

The First Christmas Carol:
Glory, glory to God
Peace, peace on earth
Goodwill, goodwill to all people.

(An old message, a new message,
a continuing message, the prophet Isaiah's message,
John the Baptist's message, our message,
a transformational leadership message:)
The voice of one crying out in the wilderness,
Prepare the way of the Lord,
Make the paths of the Lord straight.
Every valley shall be filled,
And every mountain and hill shall be made low,
And the crooked shall be made straight,
And the rough ways made smooth;
And people shall see the reign of God.
And people shall be the reign of God.

I cannot imagine telling or celebrating this lively story and message without using a variety of the arts. The story is filled with drama, action, and images. It doesn't require big budgets and a sanctuary with a large stage. It does require vision, adaptive imagination, passion, and intentional leadership to celebrate the Advent/Christmas season in a congregation's familiar worship environment and with its available resources. Not all church buildings are arts friendly, but all church buildings can be transformed into a friendly space for the arts.

The interior of Middle Collegiate Church was a traditional Protestant plan designed to focus upon the pulpit for spoken presentations and the choir loft for sung presentations. It was beautifully detailed with Tiffany windows and stenciling, brilliant gold leaf decoration, marble plaques paying tribute to persons who made important contributions to Middle's history, attractive wood outline and paneling, and delightfully themed carpeting. The space was not designed with the performing arts in mind. I loved the fact that the architecture of the sanctuary constantly challenged us to be creative, to think beyond what may have ever been done in that space before, to think "outside the box," and to use the entire space in new and inventive ways. Too many excuses for not using the performing arts in worship are directed toward a church's traditional architecture. No sanctuary was more traditional than Middle's and no sanctuary had seen a greater expression of the arts and a more imaginative use of its space.

Dancers danced on the pews, in the pews, and up and down the aisles. They danced on top of railings, on the steps leading to the pulpit, on the worship leaders' chairs, and even on the pulpit. Musicians, actors, and choirs arranged themselves in a variety of ways in, on, and among all the available spaces. Just because a church is traditional in design does not mean it has to be limiting for the use of the performing arts in the worship celebrations. Middle's sanctuary was familiar, traditional, warm, comfortable, inviting, and still we did some very exciting, surprising, spiritually uplifting and challenging, nontraditional things in this exceptionally beautiful space. It was just one more example of adaptive leadership encouraging a transformational ministry that had one foot planted in the center while the other dangled off the edge.

I confess, however, to one bizarre example of adjusting the space to better accommodate the performing arts during Sunday's worship celebrations. One person called it "a perfect example of transforming your limited space with the creative use of dirt." Soon after arriving at Middle, I wanted to include dance, a variety of musical instruments and bands, and other performances in the Sunday worship celebrations. Since the first row of pews came very close to the pulpit at the front of the sanctuary, there was no space available for groups to perform. In violation of the principle of "paying the rent" before making any significant changes, I thought of a way to remove a row of pews without anybody noticing.

Late one night after everybody left the building, with an understanding of secrecy, the sexton and I went into the sanctuary, removed the front row of pews, and carried them to a storage room on the top floor of the church house. But when we looked at the floor, there was a very clear outline of where the pews had been. The carpet was dirty and worn with age, except under the places where the pews were attached to the floor. Once the pews were removed, a clear and obvious outline was visible.

We went outside to a small garden near the entrance of the church, got a bucket of dirt, and brushed the dirt on the clean outlined areas until they matched the worn and dirty areas around it. No one ever noticed the missing pews, and now there was adequate space for dance, musical instruments, jazz bands, choirs, puppet theater, and other presentations on Sunday mornings. Later, after I had been at Middle for a while and had spent considerable time paying the rent, I told the congregation what we did. The response was laughter and applause.

The arts at Middle were not add-ons. They were not on the periphery of Middle's worship, life, and ministry. They were intentionally included in the middle of Middle. The arts played an essential role in resurrecting this once dead church back to life.

Several years ago when I walked into the Graduate Theological Union (GTU) library in Berkeley, California, I immediately noticed two things: the "Winged Figure" sculpture by Stephen DeStaebler and the space the sculpture occupies. The sculpture is in the middle of all the activity and movement within the library. Even if I entered the library singularly focused upon researching a book or a journal, I looked up to find my way and was faced with this unusual piece of art. What is it? Who is it? Why is it here instead of over there? Is it a human figure? It isn't complete. It has a wing. What about me? Am I complete or am I still evolving? Can I fly? Why am I thinking about this? I only came in here to search for an article in a journal. I am sure none of this reflection would be part of my library experience if the Winged Figure was not placed in such a central location.

This is exactly the way the arts were used at Middle Collegiate Church. I have been to churches that have concerts or house a theater or dance space or support an artist or arts group financially, but the arts are completely absent from their worship and the rest of the church's main life and programs. Like the Winged Figure placed in the center of the GTU library, the arts at Middle were intentionally placed in the middle of Middle. They were a part of the essential spirit of Middle. They were a regular and natural part of Middle's on-going worship, life, and ministry. Middle, too, supported artists and the arts financially, produced concerts, and provided space for dance and theater groups, but you would also find the arts in Middle's regular worship, education, and outreach. Because the arts were placed in such an important and central position in the middle of Middle, they played a fundamental role in the growth of Middle Church, dramatically transforming it into a growing, vibrant, and diverse congregation and one of the critically reviewed and acclaimed churches in New York City.

It was obvious that creative persons were regularly drawn to this church, located in the heart of the vibrant East Village, because of our love of and respectful attention to placing the arts in the middle of Middle. Once people became a part of the church community, they placed upon it their own artistic touch. Every year the centrality of the arts evolved and grew, constantly enriching and refining Middle's worship celebrations, and encouraging and enabling more members and participants to use their own gifts and talents.

Including the arts in worship provides a great occasion to expand the church's multicultural and multiracial participation. This is an opportunity that should not be overlooked. The effort has to be intentional, otherwise nothing will change. I worked with the director of the Middle Church Choir to insure that the membership of the choir would become and remain diverse. Whenever the jazz group was asked to play, I explained to them that the very systemic nature of Middle required that the persons playing in the group be diverse. When dance was included in the worship celebration, I made sure the choreographer understood that both the professional dancers and the volunteer adults and children from the congregation needed to be multiracial and multicultural. When we created the East Village Gospel Choir, we knew from the very beginning that it would be different from the many other gospel choirs in the city of New York—we were committed to a multiracial, multicultural, and multi-sexual orientation choir with an African-American musical tradition.

113

The very same intentional efforts went into staffing Middle's Children's AfterSchool Arts Center, the photography and art gallery exhibits, and the children and youth choirs. The key word is intentional, and intentional takes a lot of extra effort. It is much easier to include the arts without taking advantage of their terrific opportunity to assist in the diverse, multiracial, and multicultural transformation of the church. But easier is not always better.

Early one Saturday morning I was standing for a "no walk" sign on the corner of Second Avenue and 5th Street. I was dressed in a sports jacket and carrying a briefcase. In 1986 in the East Village on Saturday morning, not many people dressed in sports jackets and carried briefcases. Just before the light changed, an African-American person walked up and stood next to me, wearing a sports jacket and carrying a briefcase. We looked at each other, smiled, and he said, "I haven't seen you in the neighborhood before. I'm Rod Rodgers." I introduced myself and told him I was the new minister at Middle Collegiate Church. He said he had a dance company and their studio was a block away on East 4th Street. He invited me to stop by the studio when I had time to chat.

Later that week I called Rod and walked to the studio. I discovered he was the founder and artistic director of the Rod Rodgers Dance Company. I talked about my goal of transforming Middle Church into a diverse, multicultural, multiracial congregation with an important outreach ministry into the community and the city. He talked about how he had intentionally created a diverse multicultural, multiracial dance company with an African-American focus and choreographed dramatic social commentary in many of the dances. We immediately connected and dreamed of ways we could assist, support, and celebrate each other's efforts.

That "chance meeting" on the corner of Second Avenue and 5th Street began a long and important relationship, which had a significant impact, not only upon the arts in the worship of Middle Church, but also upon Middle's transformation into a model diverse congregation. When Rod unexpectedly died, I enhanced my efforts to comfort, support, and encourage the members of the company. Beyond an increased physical presence and spiritual efforts, I also sought out new money sources to assist them financially in the transition. It was a sad time for many of us and a difficult transition for the company. The company thrived under its new leadership and so did its relationship with Middle Church.

Over the years the Rod Rodgers Dance Company danced several Sunday sermons at Middle. The danced sermons often included their youth company. On other Sundays, individual members of the company performed prayers or participated in pieces choreographed by others. It was a great friendship and partnership with a significant contribution to the multicultural, multiracial growth and transformation of Middle Collegiate Church. The relationship was about constantly creating new entry points and opening more doors leading into the church from the community and out into the community from the church. There are never enough entry points, never enough open doors.

In 1974, two persons from the church I was serving created puppets, a frog and a toad, inspired by Arnold Lobel's award-winning Frog and Toad children's book series. When I left that church, the puppets stayed. A few years later, I was invited back to participate in an anniversary event and asked about the puppets. No one remembered when they were last used or where they were. Eventually, when the puppets were discovered in a downstairs storage area, they gave them to me. These charming characters traveled with me to Chapel Hill, North Carolina, and then to Middle Collegiate Church in New York City. An artist and interior decorator, who was working on the restoration of Middle's sanctuary, volunteered to build a stage. People in the congregation were asked to write scripts. An area fine artist created incredibly imaginative and colorful child-like props. A pianist improvised music for the productions. Approximately every six to eight weeks a new play was scheduled. Each performance was only eight minutes long, was usually humorous, and had an important message about friendship, life, and relationships. These were not your typical church or Sunday school puppet performances. They were quality theater productions, often with professional actors from the congregation. A long list of volunteers signed up to participate in the productions as either puppeteers or props assistants. Frog and Toad performances were extremely popular with both the children and adults. I was always surprised that attendance at the Sunday worship celebrations regularly increased when Frog and Toad were advertised to appear. It was a humbling experience to be upstaged by two puppets. But it shows the attraction of the arts in worship to draw new volunteers and people into the life and ministry of the church.

There is little that is more distracting to a worshipper and unattractive to a visitor than a liturgy that does not flow from a planned beginning to an intentional ending, arts that are placed as fillers, sermons that drag on with multiple beginnings and endings, and leaders who move about purposelessly. Producing a worship celebration, as well as other events and programs, is so important, that I often identified the task of producer as the main function of my ministry.

Minister as producer is a skill that all transformational leaders need to develop.

Chapter Thirteen

Minister as Producer
Another identity not taught in seminary

Seminary never explored such helpful concepts as schmoozer or doorman or producer to describe the essential roles of a minister. Even in my own mind, I felt I was preparing for something much greater. But now I look back on more than forty years of ministry and I am confronted with a very humble realization. No matter how high and lofty a ministry I anticipated when I began, my calling was always much simpler: to be a schmoozer, to love, embrace, enjoy, welcome, and accept all people; to be a doorman, opening the church doors for all of God's beautiful diversity of people and continuously opening ever more diverse entry points into the church, greeting, welcoming, serving, being a church concierge; and to be a producer, seeing to it that every aspect of the church's worship celebration fit into a flow from beginning to end and that it all was consistent with the essential spirit and vision of the church. Schmoozer, doorman, producer—that's me; that was my calling; that was my ministry.

It was a more modest calling and ministry than I anticipated.

If a church is to be a growing, multiple-entry church filled with God's beautiful human diversity, it must be intentional or it won't happen. I cannot repeat that enough. If the performing arts are to be used within the Sunday morning worship celebration, it must be intentional; otherwise, church leaders will opt for the much easier route of sticking with the traditional printed and verbal liturgies. If the language of justice and a variety of people and gifts are to be included in the worship celebrations, it must be intentional, or the language of culture will prevail while the language of the church remains static. This is the work of minister as producer—to purposefully care for the content and flow of the total worship so the verbal and non-verbal elements and the timing of each all work together.

I have had the opportunity to attend enough worship celebrations where it was quite obvious to me the clergy and other worship leaders didn't have a clue about minister as producer. Yes, the performing arts were included, but it felt like the arts were present just to fill space between the more important verbal parts of the worship. It felt like the arts were included to provide decoration; they were inserted for show or to interpret the verbal. Minister as producer understands the integrity and importance of non-verbal ways of communicating and perceiving.

I now frequently attend worship in several different churches located in a variety of settings. In some, the flow of the celebration seems a bit awkward. There is a beginning, a middle, an end, and then what feels like a beginning again followed by a second ending. Or there may be a beginning and middle, and then what feels like another beginning. Minister as producer sees to it that the worship celebration has a consistent movement from one beginning to one ending.

I attended a special event worship celebration during which there were to be several verbal interfaith presentations along with innovative multicultural and interfaith dance and music presentations. I arrived early in anticipation of such diversity and creativity. It began with an incredibly moving and spiritually celebrative dance performance. Then a person came forward to introduce the speakers. He spoke for thirty-five minutes, just to introduce the primary speakers of the event. The placing and timing of that worship celebration was completely out of whack from the very beginning. It was obvious that the arts were included just to fill gaps in what were going to be unbearably long verbal presentations. I got up and walked out, and I wasn't the only one. Minister as producer watches over the timing and placing of each element within the celebration. A dance, song, music, verbal speech, or theater piece placed at one point will be something quite different placed at another point, and the length of each element is important to the timing of each other element and of the whole. Clear communication between the producer and participants is critical. During any given worship celebration, there may be many persons whose responsibility it is to take care of their own individual participation, such as inside space, outside space, music, songs, choir, dance, movement, theater, speaker, sermon, prayers, lights, sound, programs, greeters, offering, etc., but the minister as producer's responsibility is to take care of the whole and to care for the whole of the congregation, as well as her or his own individual participation.

Watching out for the language used in the total worship celebration is another task of minister as producer. Judith Rock makes the point that paying attention to the language of worship is "a matter of theological process rather than personal preference."[24] There was a time in the 1970s and 80s when worship leaders seemed more sensitive to the language used in worship. In the 1990s and beyond, it appears like we've lost much of our sensitivity to the meaning and theology of the language used on Sunday mornings. Inclusive language concerns should have been settled a long time ago. There is no reason why we should still be addressing language issues. Language matters. Words matter. Language evolves. Words evolve. What specific words and phrases meant in years past is not what they necessarily mean today and what they will mean tomorrow. Is that too complex for worship leaders in our churches to comprehend? Doing away with language that is either overtly or subtly sexist, militaristic, violent, anti-Semitic, homophobic, etc. in a worship celebration is not a matter of personal choice; it is a matter of justice, faith, and theology. If the language used in worship teaches or models something other than the Gospel, it should not be used. That seems very simple to me, although years of experience has shown me it is hard work, very time-consuming, and sensitive to change the language of worship. It is the responsibility of minister as producer to fashion worship that remains a part of the historic Christian tradition and "yet is genuinely responsive to the present cultural environment and is accessible, attractive, and hospitable to all who are outside the church."[25] Minister as producer takes care of all the big and little details in the worship celebration that will make it

---

[24] Rock, *Performer as Priest & Prophet,* p. 20.

[25] Thomas G. Long, *Beyond the Worship Wars: Building Vital and Faithful Worship,* (The Alban Institute, 2001), p. 11.

possible for the church to "create a new thing in the earth."[26]

Most often the move from sexist language to inclusive language in the worship celebration means everything has to be adapted or rewritten, and at times that means taking a close look at some of the most "sacred" and traditional items in the liturgy. An example is The Lord's Prayer. What about the words "Father" and "kingdom?" How appropriate are they, given today's meaning and imagery? Something I found to be very meaningful in my ministry at Middle Collegiate Church was to change the prayer to: "Ever-loving God, Hallowed be Your name, Your reign come, Your will be done, on earth as it is in heaven. Give us this day our daily bread. Forgive us our sins as we forgive those who sin against us. And lead us not into temptation, but deliver us from evil. For Yours is the reign, and the power, and the glory, forever. Amen." Even after using this version for several years, some staff and others still felt they needed to explain or defend it.

My priority was to boldly model the prayer as a part of the church's essential justice ministry, and if some in the congregation wanted to say it differently, fine. The change has to do with the core Gospel message of justice, and has nothing to do with tradition or with the way we have always said it before or believing the words spoken don't really make any difference. We know better than that. The words we speak do make a difference. The words we use are important. The words we use teach and model and nurture. Justice is central to the Gospel. No Bible translation has the original version of The Lord's Prayer, anyway. All the different Bibles used are from versions originated and copied from texts years re-

---

[26] Ibid., p. 12

moved from the original texts.[27] To be consistent with using inclusive language in our worship is hard work. Justice is hard work. We have to work boldly and purposefully at it, all the time. Maybe that is why many clergy and church leaders avoid inclusive language. Once the commitment is made to move away from language in our worship celebrations that is sexist, militaristic, violent, anti-Semitic, homophobic, etc., we need to be aware that we are starting down a long, difficult road that will ultimately lead us to examine, adapt, and change almost everything we say, print, sing, and publicly read. That is just the way it is, no matter how many arguments or excuses are made to keep things as they are. It certainly isn't the first, nor will it be the last, justice concern church leaders choose to detour.

A joy of minister as producer is the many opportunities to work in partnership with other professional and volunteer persons. A Lone Ranger style of leadership may at times appear appealing, but it won't work for the duration of the transformation process.

---

[27] Cf. Bart D. Ehrman, *Misquoting Jesus: The Story Behind Who Changed the Bible and Why,* (HarperSanFrancisco, 2005).

Chapter Fourteen

Don't Go It Alone
The Lone Ranger style of leadership doesn't work

Don't go it alone is recommended for all aspects of transformational leadership. It is a mistake to go it alone when leading a congregation through a time of change and transformation. The Lone Ranger style of leadership is a sure prescription for a short-term ministry with few important accomplishments. An essential priority for effective transformational leadership is to gather and develop trusted colleagues and a network of partners and, at the same time, remain in contact with those who disagree with the new vision for the church. At Middle, it was obvious a sea-change needed to happen or the funeral dirge would soon ring from the belfry. It is best never to make any big moves or significant changes until a supportive coalition is developed that cannot be blocked. "It is not enough to point to a hopeful future. People need to know that you know what you are asking them to give up on the way to creating a better future."[28] Communicating, understanding, embracing, networking, building a coalition, knowing where people are at, and schmoozing are all important transformational leadership qualities. The ability to remain friends with supporters and opponents alike, and to know where both stand, is critical.

To make the changes necessary to bring a stuck and struggling church back to life, nothing can replace a positive partnership with members of the official board. It is a mistake to misjudge the importance of bringing the board along in transforming the church. My charge was to bring new life out of a dysfunctional life, purpose out of chaos, and leadership where leaders didn't lead. But not even members of the board were prepared for the changes and loss that needed to occur before they could experience their hoped for vision of the resurrection of their beloved church.

The early meetings with the board were mostly friendly, but were frequently tense. They were always filled with lively discussion, which often generated polite arguments. At times, I was filled with hope and anticipation, and at other times, I felt discouraged and frustrated. I usually left the meetings still feeling called to see the entire journey through to the end, but there were some nights when I felt like running. Going it alone or abandoning the process, however, were not options. I remembered the words of the psychologist: "You were chosen for this ministry because you are a survivor."

Over time, more and more of us found our individual voices within a shared vision. This shared vision was constantly repeated, rehearsed, modeled, and taught. It became a reality, first with the new growing congregation and then with

---

[28] Heifetz, *Leadership on the Line,* p. 75.

the church board itself. The principles of paying the rent are as important and critical with members of the board as they are with the general congregation. A new partnership of leaders began to emerge. Others, who could not support the new vision and emergent partnership, left the board or rotated off. Persons representing the new growing congregation came onto the board and provided critical fresh leadership, energy, and skills. The hoped for resurrection of Middle Church was happening, and we were doing it together.

Ultimately, I had incredibly supportive and skilled board chairs and chairs of the important finance task force. Each one made significant contributions to moving Middle forward in the journey toward transformation. Without these leaders stepping up to lead, the transformation of Middle would not have happened and my tenure would not have lasted for twenty years. It took seven years for the vision to be mutually owned by the leadership and the congregation, much longer than I originally anticipated, but we made it through some early desperate times together in order to later experience the joys of a diverse partnership and the fulfillment of traveling the entire journey. Going it alone would never have brought us so far on the transformational journey from there to here. It would only have added to the distractions that already existed. Although it took longer and created more work, continuously paying the rent with members of the board produced greater opportunities to lead toward a solution, instead of becoming a part of the problem. Along with the board, eager and talented volunteers formed a new leadership network that completely recreated the Middle Church congregation and ministry. The Lone Ranger style of leadership is not effective for the long term.

It is both exciting and hard work to bring a dead, stagnant, or declining church back to life. It takes a lot of mental, emotional, spiritual, and physical energy. Not many leaders who attempt to go it alone make it. They start looking for another church as soon as they hit the first bump in the road. Good friendships are important. The right colleagues are important. A supportive board is important. Enthusiastic volunteers excited about helping to carry out the new vision are important. People who will speak the truth in love are important. It is great to have cheerleaders, mentors, supporters, and encouragers along the way. Always reading, learning, growing, and being open to adventurous and new experiences are important. It may also take more financial resources and specific expertise than what is often available at the beginning of some transformational journeys.

It is not helpful for a church to go it alone at this stage either. Leaders need to search out partnerships with other larger churches which have greater resources, network with compatible organizations or groups, research available grants and foundations, solicit funds from a broader list of possible outside donors, consider establishing separate non-profit corporations, and explore a host of other appropriate outreach and fundraising possibilities.

To help leaders build effective transformational teams, Lovett Weems describes nine qualities that should be present when putting a team together: treat everyone with respect, involve people, foster collaboration, strengthen others through sharing power, communicate, be with the people, recognize people, develop others, and love the people.[29] The transformation of a congregation will have a greater chance of success if both the church leaders and the church itself do

---

[29] Weems, *Church Leadership,* pp. 75-90.

not attempt to go it alone. It is also important for churches to support, encourage, and partner with one another.

At the beginning of Middle's Easter journey, limited financial resources did not allow for hiring experienced people to the church's staff, and a declining and chaotic church environment didn't leave much of a volunteer pool. I relied mostly on part-time seminarian assistance and other task-specific staffing to lead individual programs and carry out particular tasks. Later, some of these positions and tasks were filled by more permanent full-time and part-time people, both lay and ordained. When the church began to grow, more volunteers were recruited for critical positions and tasks.

Selecting administrative, clergy associates, and music staff are some of the most important decisions a senior transformational leader can make. Colleagues who have a positive attitude, share the vision, know how to function in a team ministry, and are capable of taking the initiative to do what they were brought in to do are essential assets to bringing a dying church back to life. On the other hand, colleagues who have a negative attitude, don't ever learn how to function on a team, bring too much personal baggage to the workplace, and cannot get started on their own to do the work they were called to do can create extra work for the senior minister and the board, drain attention and energy from the real vision, and even stall or detour the transformational journey. Selecting the right people with the right fit is critical because firing or assisting a person to move on to another job or terminating a volunteer can be difficult, time-consuming, painful, and cause unnecessary distractions.

It was my practice whenever meeting people or visiting a seminary or attending an event in the community or church to always listen, be alert, observe, and write down names of people who were possible future colleagues and candidates for available positions at Middle. I always had an ongoing list of people I had already informally observed in regard to friendliness, spirit, quality of person and work, diversity needed at Middle, compatibility, and so on. This practice helped bring to Middle's staff several very talented, creative, and quality people who were essential in advancing Middle's reinvention.

Occasionally, the process did not work and a completely wrong person was invited to join the staff. It happens. Even though every person's contract, including my own, said we were hired "at will," firing or letting a staff person go can be difficult and very disrupting.

Once we hired a full-time associate minister who, after two years on the job, insisted that her contract be changed to include many of the same responsibilities of the senior minister. Duplication of work by members of the staff is a waste of time and energy, poor use of limited financial resources, shortchanges the vision, undermines a team concept, and causes stress with the other staff. It was a long and difficult process for her to move on to another place and position. During the process, we lost four active members who felt the person was treated unfairly.

There is no such thing as an unimportant paid or volunteer position in a church's ministry. Every selection is as important to the total vision as the next and needs to be treated that way. Staffing is a critical part of what it means to not go it alone in the journey to resurrect a dying church.

Another significant consideration is how does a leader in the midst of the demands of bringing a stagnant or dead church back to life renew one's own spirit and refresh one's own growth with new ideas and creativity? For me, it was a commitment to a one day weekly holiday away from the local work environment. It was the inner pull of being by, on, and in a body of water. It was the fascination of discovering new authors, exploring adventurous ideas, and imagining challenging new possibilities. It was the consistency of family relationships and the family's support of the vision. It was also having friendships beyond the local life, work, and relationships.

It is rare for a transformational leader to be able to sustain the required spirit, creativity, imagination, and growth through local involvement and relationships alone. Broader networks beyond the local that support, cheerlead, challenge, and encourage are not only important, but necessary.

Satisfying my spirit came from many different broader sources, but most notably from a thirty-year relationship with Doug, Professor of Christianity and the Arts at the Pacific School of Religion, and the Center for Arts, Religion, and Education (C.A.R.E.) in Berkeley, California. Attending conferences, leading workshops, teaching courses, participating in lengthy conversations on religion, the arts, and politics, and enjoying unguarded friendship in a different environment constantly refreshed my spirit and inspired me to even greater adventures in transformational leadership. The local context was satisfying; it was my calling and commitment, but I also needed the broader contacts to more fully fill my spirit and sustain my growth for the duration of the difficult transformational journey.

The broader picture was always essentially connected with the local context. The two were never separated; the one always fed the other. On many occasions, Doug brought a creative and imaginative presence to Middle's worship celebrations. He preached sermons as first person Henry Ward Beecher and John Calvin. He once gave a sermon while standing on a pew in the front row. He would sometimes walk up and down the center aisle while speaking, occasionally stopping to address a particular person directly. I consulted with Doug from the beginning of my time at Middle and he was often present to aid me in whatever ways were helpful. He encouraged, celebrated, and cheered every new advance Middle made toward transformation. He never tired in uplifting the congregation, congratulating them for sustaining the transformation journey, telling them what a wonderful and important thing they were doing, and always promoting Middle Church to a broader national audience. Together Doug and I started an innovative C.A.R.E. Arts Ministry NYC intercession course at Middle in which twenty-five students from the Graduate Theological Union came to New York City every January. It was co-hosted by C.A.R.E. and Middle Collegiate Church. Doug was my personal cheerleader and a partner in Middle's resurrection who inspired and challenged us to keep on keeping on, bringing a dying church back to an adventurous and unconventional new life and constantly breaching the barriers of what a church can be.

One of the great joys of church leadership are the many opportunities we have for networking, partnering, building coalitions, supporting, celebrating with others, and working with a broad diversity of people who have a wide range of skills, talents, interests, contacts, and energy. It is a mistake for transformational leaders to ignore these resources. Church leaders' first instinct is to go it alone. Remember, the best advice is, "don't go it alone, the Lone Ranger style of leadership doesn't work."

Throughout many of the chapters, familiar biblical stories were retold as models of transformational leadership. Chapter Fifteen takes this essential principle one step further and illustrates how the stories not only model, but also shape the role of leader in turning around a static or declining congregation. In my own ministry, these biblical stories provided spiritual inspiration and foundation for all the other transformational building blocks.

Chapter Fifteen

Biblical Stories That Shape the Role of Leader in Congregational Transformation

There are many biblical stories that have had a profound and continuing impact upon my life and ministry. The stories have also continued to raise important questions that helped me develop new ideas and practical insights into the role of transformational leadership. Some people read the Bible and get answers; I read the Bible and get questions that confront me and nudge me toward change and new life. Challenging questions have always been in the front and center of my faith. Over the years I have learned to welcome and trust these questions of faith, life, and leadership. "Be patient toward all that is unsolved in your heart," writes the poet Rainer Maria Rilke. "And try to love the questions themselves. Do not seek the answers that cannot be given you because you would not be able to live them. And the point is to live everything. Live the questions now."

I divided the biblical stories and the important questions from these stories into two groups. The first group is a series of six stories that have impacted my own story and influenced my understanding of transformational leadership. The second group is a series of biblical stories describing a Christ-style life-journey which provided the spiritual foundation, under-standing, and encouragement for resurrecting Middle Collegiate Church to new life.

The first group begins with the account of the Great Banquet in which Jesus tells the story of a person who pre-pared a magnificent banquet and invited all the regular and correct folks, but each guest had an excuse for not attending. So the party-giver went out into the region and invited every-one—no matter who, no matter what, no questions asked, no requirements necessary. He pushed the doors to the banquet room wide open and created a multitude of new entrance points into the Great Banquet so all the diverse people of the region could join the festivities. What I got from this story is that excluding and constructing doctrines, policy, theology, and liturgy to determine who is in and who is out is wrong. Welcoming people is the Gospel and is fundamental to bring-ing new life to a tired or ailing church.

In the story of the Good Samaritan, Jesus talks of a per-son who was going happily on his way when he came upon a victim of violence. The story isn't all that unusual, except that the victim was someone who the person disliked both his-torically and traditionally; someone the person couldn't stand; someone with whom the person never associated. Neverthe-less, he bathed and bandaged the victim's wounds, took him to an inn, and stayed overnight to help him out. This act of compassion, generosity, and love toward the victim, the stereotyped, the stranger, the one who is different, is the bib-lical definition of moral humanity. The Good Samaritan story reminded me that disregarding and avoiding people because they are different from us and have different experiences, traditions, beliefs, and history from our own is wrong. What I took away from this story is that assisting, accepting, and loving people is the Gospel and is an important leadership quality when transforming the worship and life of a church.

During my entire adult years I have been deeply moved by the Sarah and Abraham story. By faith these two senior citizens set out on their spiritual journey, not knowing where it would take them. No biblical personalities have had more impact upon my life and ministry. The story reminded me of the question, "How did I ever get here from there?" Faith, risking, journeying, making a decision without having to be sure about the outcome; going forward with one's faith and life, not knowing where the journey will lead; and going where there is no path, have all influenced my own spirituality, faith, decisions, and willingness to trust the journey and risk the adventure. There was a poster hanging on the wall of the Kirkridge Retreat and Study Center in Bangor, Pennsylvania that said: "Don't travel where the path leads, rather, go where there is no path ... and leave a trail." That is exactly what Sarah and Abraham did, and they sure did leave a trail. I have been dedicated to following their example my entire adult life. "There is no freeway to the future. No paved highway from here to tomorrow. There is only wilderness. Only uncertain terrain. There are no road maps. No signposts. So pioneering leaders rely upon a compass and a dream."[30] "Going out not knowing" defines the very essence of faith and is a basic principle of congregational transformation.

A great source of spiritual encouragement and challenge

---

[30] James M. Kouzes and Barry Z. Posner, *The Leadership Challenge,* (Jossey-Bass, San Francisco, 1988), p. 89.

was the story of "creating a new thing in the earth," located in two different books of the Bible. The vision in Revelation of a new heaven and a new earth is an important vision for transformational leaders. And in Isaiah, "Behold, I am making all things new. It is already happening. Can you perceive it?" When I was a new church start minister or whenever I was beginning the process of renewing a declining established congregation, I always asked the question, "What does it mean to create something new, not simply transplant something old into a new place and time?" To transform an ailing or dying church is about "creating a new thing in the earth" and not about wasting time and energy discovering how to do better what the church has always been doing. The biblical vision is a new heaven and a new earth. The critical faith declaration and question is, "It is already happening. Can you perceive it?"

I have mentioned elsewhere in the book the story in Ezekiel. Here I want to emphasize the importance of the question in the story, "Can these dry bones live again?" This is the question that needs to be on the lips of every leader who walks through the doors of a dying church feeling called by God to resurrect the church to new life, "Can these dry bones live again?" And God said: "I am going to put my renewing, refreshing Spirit within you, and you will be alive, and you will live, and you will be vital and dynamic again!" "Can these dry bones live again?" "Sure they can. Sure they can. No bones about it." That response formed the essence and confidence of how I approached a dying Middle Collegiate Church. It is impossible for me to recall how many times Ezekiel's question and God's answer encouraged me in Middle's transformational journey.

A story in Deuteronomy filled my mind and spirit with a

138

celebratory visual image of Miriam leading the people in worship with joy, dance, and percussion instruments. It is an early biblical account of using the performing arts in worship. In the tradition of Miriam, I have always had a soft spot in worship for dance and celebration. Yes, it's okay to dance, play drums, clap hands, sway to the music, and be joyous and thankful in church. It is a grand biblical tradition. Every Sunday public worship is a "little Easter" celebration and should not be confused with or patterned after the way we conduct our private devotions and meditations.

I was not surprised that this first group of six stories inspired and encouraged the journey of resurrecting Middle Church to new life. What *was* surprising to me is how frequently I thought of these accounts as stories about transformational leadership. I didn't expect that. I didn't intentionally search the Bible for clues about transformational, adaptive leadership. That was often the last thing I was thinking about. But there it was; I couldn't ignore it. "Are many of the biblical stories about transformational, adaptive leadership?" I ask. "Is leadership about leading? Yes, I think so."

The next group of biblical stories form what I call the Christ-style life-journey. They are the Holy Week stories of Palm Sunday, Maundy Thursday, Good Friday, and Easter. Each event in Jesus' "Holy Week" life leads one step closer to Easter. Easter is the goal of transformation. Transformation in the life of a congregation is an Easter experience, and there is no shortcut to Easter. For a congregation to reach an Easter resurrection it must first go the entire transformational journey through Palm Sunday, Maundy Thursday, and Good Friday.

The Palm Sunday story in the Gospel by Luke, Chapter Nineteen, is about vision and following a plan to carry out the vision. Vision is where the transformational process begins

139

and Palm Sunday is where Jesus intentionally enters the road that leads to Easter. In the story, Jesus chose to ride on a donkey into the city that is a center of religious and political authority. Some of the people gathered in the city were hoping for the emergence of a leader to deliver them from the hardship of this authority. Maybe it would be Jesus. But why was he riding on a donkey? What was the meaning of this? Where were the horses and chariots? Where were the Humvees and airplanes? What kind of leader was this? Was it a different way? Was it a new idea? The people were not expecting this! It all seemed too non-violent, too ordinary, too peaceful! There the people stood, confronted by a new vision and challenged to choose the things that will lead to life, not death. Some along the way were handed palm branches and spread them on the road. As Jesus passed by following the road signs that pointed in the direction of Easter, people wondered and began to wander off in different directions.

The Palm Sunday story is about intentional, transformational leadership. It is about discovering a new vision, taking a risk, taking a stand, going into the center of life and community, and acting our conscience to do what is right. In the midst of stagnation, decay, decline, and near death, the rider on the donkey ignites the spark of a glorious anticipated new time, a vision of a fresh way, a glimpse of a new congregation, a new city, a new world. "Rejoice, rejoice … your deliverer is coming … riding into the center of a troubled existence on a donkey!" "Can you perceive it?" Transformational leaders intentionally lead toward change, Easters, new life.

In the Gospel by John, Chapter Thirteen, is one of the versions of Maundy Thursday. On the Thursday before Easter Jesus said to his disciples and friends: "I have set for you a life-example. It is a duty, an obligation, a non-negotiable, that you now do for others what I have done for you. I tell you the truth, no one person, race, ethnic background, gender, age, sexual-orientation, economic status, and nation is greater than any other. Now that you know this truth of love, community, and relationship, how happy you and all humankind will be when you put it into practice." That is the mandate of Maundy in Maundy Thursday. That is the non-negotiable of our faith. That is what makes the Thursday before Easter holy. The Maundy Thursday decision is either for maintaining the status-quo, doing more of the same, or for going with Jesus on a journey into Easter, new life, new possibilities, a transformed existence with a new vision, fully aware that the journey will lead us straight through the struggle, pain, chaos, loss, and dying of the old of Good Friday. The painful Maundy Thursday reality of the transformational process is that no resurrected new life happens without first the dying of the old life. There are many stories of declining and ailing churches who will call a new minister hoping she or he will turn their church around into a new life and time, but the church boards don't want to let go of their old, declining ways of doing things. A resurrected new life will never happen for them. All the roads leading into Easter experiences go through Good Friday experiences. The critical Maundy Thursday decision is to "keep on keeping on." To stay the course toward Easter is an essential ingredient to transformational leadership.

The Roman authorities had enough of this Jew who continued to adapt traditional religion and politics into a more loving and inclusive way. They ordered him to be put to death by crucifixion. The church called this event Good Friday. In Luke's account of Good Friday in Chapter Twenty-three, Jesus says with a loud voice, "Mother/Father God, into your hands I commend my spirit." Having said this, Jesus died.

The faith challenge is to follow Jesus' lead all the way through our own difficult Good Fridays of the dying of the old into our own transforming Easters of the rising of the new. Through the Good Friday story, Jesus pursued a vision of a new heaven and a new earth, where people didn't have to become immobile by old fears, prejudices, and the same old ways of doing things, which keep getting the same old results. Good Fridays precede Easters. The rising of the new emerges out of the dying of the old. There is no other way into Easter. Traveling with our lives and our congregations through the loss, chaos, and pain of Good Fridays toward the resurrection and new life of Easters is the single most difficult part of the journey for transformational, adaptive leaders. Middle Church's Good Friday meant everything had to change before Middle could experience the resurrection of new life. Middle's Good Friday meant loss of people, recognizable worship, and familiar ways of doing things. Letting go so Easters could happen at Middle was hard, chaotic, and painful.

Luke's Easter story is recorded in Chapter Twenty-four. "On the first day of the week, at early dawn, the women came to the tomb. They found the stone rolled away from the tomb, but when they went in, they did not find the body. While they were perplexed about this, suddenly two people dressed in dazzling clothes stood beside them. The women were terrified and bowed their faces to the ground, but the two said to them, 'Why do you look for the living among the dead? Jesus is not here, but has risen.'" Imagine, Easters. Imagine, bringing new life to a stagnant, declining, or dead church. Imagine, resurrection. Transformational leaders imagine. The foundation of transformational, adaptive leadership is imagining Easters. No matter how much my rational side pulls and tugs at me, deep in my being I believe and have experienced the good news, the next opportunity, the better future, the transformational message of Easter which has the miraculous potential of keeping faith and hope alive. The great thing about the Easter story is that Easter encourages us to imagine, envision, hope, and do more than we can ever know. Easters are times to rediscover and reclaim once again what is possible—not impossible—in this life, time, and place we are given to live. Easters are opportunities to invest ourselves in envisioning the divine promise of a wildly new day, time, and place. If we are not able in these times to imagine Easters in life, churches, institutions, organizations, and the world, then we may be holding on far too tightly to what we know and to the way things are. The real question is: can we, will we dare to let Easters happen for us and for our churches as it did for those on the first Easter? Easters. Vision. Imagination. Change. Transformation. New Life. It is a continuous goal of an ongoing and intentional journey. Transformational leaders lead through the entire journey. They don't let up or lose momentum or bail out halfway through the process. The Gospel is about transformational, adaptive leadership and leadership is following Jesus' example of leading through the entire journey.

This transformational leadership model is a Christ-style life-journey: from Palm Sunday, to Maundy Thursday, through Good Friday, to Easter. It follows Jesus' life-journey through the events of Holy Week. It begins in the Palm Sunday challenge of entering into the center of life, into the center of the world, doing our duty, acting our consciences, fulfilling our obligation to do what is right for others. From there Jesus' spiritual life-journey continues in Maundy Thursday's decision not to turn back, but to "keep on keeping on" toward Easter, into the Good Friday brokenness of the dying of the old and, ultimately, into the wholeness of the Easter rising of the new. This Christ-style life-journey is an intentional and ongoing transformational, adaptive process. It is the foundation for a positive change leadership model, which continuously travels the entire journey through to Easters. The Christ-style life-journey formed the spiritual foundation for understanding and leading the incredible resurrection of Middle Collegiate Church.

This inspiring resurrection was the result of a great supportive and encouraging partnership between professional leaders, volunteer leaders, congregations, and official boards. We all did what we said we would do. Of course, the new challenge is, "be careful what you ask for."

Chapter Sixteen

A Great Partnership
We did what we said we would do

In 1996, *The New York Times* ran a large feature article about my ministry at Middle. The next week, this letter arrived in the mail from the psychologist who interviewed me for the search committee eleven years earlier: "I so much enjoyed reading the positive things *The New York Times* had to say about your ministry. Every time I hear how well you are doing (which is often) I feel a little charge of pride at having had a hand in your being at Middle Collegiate. Congratulations on receiving such a wonderful write-up—and for doing such a wonderful job." Survived. Thrived. Called. I guaranteed it.

My commitment to the Collegiate Church was the guarantee to resurrect a new, creative, growing, vital congregation at Middle Collegiate Church—one that was more completely and systemically diverse than Collegiate had ever seen in its over 375 year history in the city of New York. Their commitment to me was to forget about closing the church, support me and a positive birth of a new congregation and ministry at Second Avenue and 7th Street, restore the building to its historic beauty, and equip the facility for a twenty-first century ministry. For twenty years, we had a great partnership and a terrific run together. Bringing a dead church back to life would not have happened without this partnership. We kept focused on the vision and we both kept our commitments to one another.

Early in Collegiate's search process, I toured the Middle Collegiate Church facility. It was obvious the church house and the sanctuary had been neglected for years and that critical maintenance had been deferred, perhaps waiting for the inevitable closing of the church. Roofs were leaking, plaster was falling down, walls and floors were cluttered, dirty, and dark, the office was chaotic, the kitchen was small and outdated, and the bathrooms smelled.

Middle's building will always be an evolving work in progress as the congregation, ministry, community, and city constantly change. Part of the building's attractiveness is that it is a traditional structure in which so many exciting, new, and non-traditional things happen. One does not have to throw the traditional away in order to birth a new, imaginative ministry. One does, however, have to be creative enough to constantly use the old space in completely new ways. The East Village, and even the city, changed and evolved every five-to-seven years. The real challenge was for the church and the church's leaders to stay relevant and fresh within such a dynamic environment. Stagnation, irrelevance, and decline can happen very quickly and sometimes go unnoticed for years.

I personally, spiritually, and professionally traveled a long distance in my extensive and blessed ministry, but I found a home in New York City and at Middle Collegiate Church. I loved the city, the East Village, and Middle Church. It was there where I found love, friendship, and freedom to stretch the boundaries of what a church can be. I also found there an invigorating and generous protection from the craziness that denominations, boards, and communities can sometimes inflict upon transformational, adaptive leaders. I will forever be grateful to the Collegiate Church, the board, and its senior ministers, and to Middle's congregation and board for the unbelievably wonderful and challenging twenty-year ministry and time in New York City. We did it together. We went the entire journey. Together, with one foot planted in the center and the other dangling off the edge, we did bring a dead church back to incredible new and unconventional life.

Chapter Seventeen

Leaders Need to Grow Spiritually, Too
Two prayers, a psalm, and a song

I've made plenty of mistakes in life and ministry, and I've celebrated blessed success. I know that transformational, adaptive leadership begins from the inside. I've been around the church long enough to have seen too many leaders exhibiting exceptional outward skills, but an obvious unexamined inside. "Leaders who can be trusted to guide the evolution of institutions into the future will be those who lead well-examined lives."[31] Reinventing a church is very difficult and spiritually draining. It is easy to become part of the problem or a distraction or even the focus of the problem, instead of the solution. When a leader is being criticized or challenged, it is often difficult to distinguish between the role of transformational leader and the self. It is important not to get the role and the self confused, otherwise all criticism and conflict will become so internalized as to jeopardize the ability to lead. To

---

[31] Granberg-Michaelson, *Leadership from Inside Out,* p. 17.

remain an effective leader in leading the resurrection of Middle Collegiate Church from near death, it was imperative to constantly examine who I was and to regularly put my own spirituality and person in perspective. As one who was leading Middle's transformation, I had to also care for my own transformation. Included here are two prayers, a Psalm, and a song that have been helpful to me in sustaining regular self-examination and spiritual growth.

Gordon's Prayer

This is a prayer first written in 1986 and revised weekly throughout my twenty years at Middle Church. The journalistic character of the prayer served as a continuous and evolving connection between God, my inner being, and my human and spiritual yearnings. The prayer is shared here as a model, an example, and a reminder for transformational leaders to be intentional about living constantly examined lives.

Ever-loving God
You blessed me with
  parents who were religious, innovative
  open, generous and encouraging
I am forever thankful and indebted to you
  and to them.
You called me as a child
  It is a sacred blessing
  I have dearly held all my life.
God, we saw one another, face to face
You called me to be an apostle
  in the long line of apostles from biblical
  times to the present.

You called me in a simple child-like vision
   that is constantly in my memory
   and positively impacts
   who I am and what I am always becoming.
I was vulnerable in my youth and you protected me.
   I struggled all the way
   I fought you
   I fought everyone in authority
   and I fought myself.
I could not run fast enough
   that you did not catch up with me
   I could not hide good enough
   that you did not find me.
You pursued me
   with goodness and mercy
You persisted to lead me
   on paths which have
   constantly challenged me
   to go beyond my own abilities
   beyond my childhood environment
   beyond my learning
   and early life experiences.
The journey is constant, and is still.
Sometimes I yearn for
   people, places and times of the past
   and there are moments
   when I wish for a more quiet
   settled, "normal" life.
My person, life and faith have been characterized
   by a restlessness that cannot be calmed
   dreams that cannot be realized
   questions that cannot find answers

friendships that cannot satisfy an aloneness
elder years that cannot match what I had imagined.
I often yearn for more inner peace
I constantly struggle with my person and life
but I have accepted my calling
and who I am.
You never allowed me
to go back or to settle in
or to be "ordinary"
or to do only the "expected"
or to journey only the well-traveled roads.
Nor could I
Nor can I
Nor will I
I have risked too much,
I have experienced too much
I have changed too much
I have journeyed too much
I believe too much.
So I continue to press on
with one foot planted firmly in the center
and the other dangling off the edge
to fulfill my calling
to reach out broader
to stretch out wider
to spread out more inclusively
to open more doors
to welcome more people
to celebrate an ever-expanding diversity
to be grateful for the Lord of the Dance
to rescue worship and religion
from becoming too boring and too irrelevant

and to be in awe of your Amazing Grace
   in the middle of it all.
Like the branches of the tree blowing in the wind
   you have constantly faced me toward the edge
   yet like the trunk of a huge oak
   you have planted my roots
   deep into the center.
You have blessed me with family
   who know me through and through
   and love me still, and all.
   I often wish I was
   a better husband
   a better father
   a better grandfather.
   I love my family, dearly
   I am thankful, constantly
   I try hard, sincerely
   we have been through it all
   and still are forgiving, loving
   family, best friends, travelers together
   they fill my days with loving friendship
   deep gratitude, abiding pride, and guiding direction
   my hope is that I will be able to build upon
   the example of my own parents: generous
   accepting, forgiving, encouraging.
   I live on in later years
   confident that my family relationships
   although not without difficult times
   have, nevertheless, been good enough.
   As time goes on
   and my days seem more numbered
   I worry more about family

and also feel more blessed by each person.
Middle Collegiate Church
is the pride of my ministry
twenty years in
a historic place
an important time
in a sometimes troubled and targeted city
   yet still beautiful, resilient, and great city
   with so many doors to open
   so many people to welcome
   so many spiritual needs to fill
   so many distractions demanding attention
   so many interruptions to which to respond
   so many individual differences to balance
   with so few gifts to offer
   so few talents with which to serve.
My prayer every week is
God, don't abandon me now
we have gone too far together
the distance has been too long
the journey too overwhelming
the task is great
I try to do the best I can
   with what I have and
   with who I am
my energy and skills are limited.

By your grace and mercy
   all my life I have overachieved
   for you, for others
   and for the good of the church
As the years progressed in ministry

I felt more tired
  sometimes even weary
doing ministry on the edge
   "creating a new thing in the earth"
  for so many years took their toll.
My prayer is always
  may your Spirit, loving God
  continuously refresh my soul
  and revive my person
  and give me the insight to know
  and the grace to accept
  the timing of my time.
 Ministry in New York City is
  so pressure-inducing and energy-draining
  so confronting and challenging
  so exciting and exhilarating
  so filled with possibilities and creativity
  I would not exchange these years
  in this great city for anything else
  or for any other place.
No matter where
  my life-journey takes me
  and no matter where I may
  temporarily reside
  this neighborhood
  this city and
  Middle Church will always be my home
  in my heart
  in my spirit
  no matter what
  no matter where.
I find myself constantly searching for

the water of the River of Life
that flows through
the middle of the city
through the middle of Middle
through the middle of me.
God, as I walk the streets
of this neighborhood and city I love
(so far from where my journey started)
        how did I ever get here, from there,
        but by your grace and your Calling.
As I connect with
    the city's beautiful mosaic of diverse
    peoples, lifestyles, cultures, races
    sexual orientations, faiths, creativity
as I become energized
in this place
of heightened energy and expression
continue to reassure me of your joy
    toward the ministry I do
continue to show me your face
continue to give me the confidence
    of your divine presence
    like you did when I was a small child
calling me then
while traveling on a Sunday afternoon
along an isolated country road in rural Michigan
and now calling me while traveling each day along
the active streets of this great city
to be an apostle to all people
who feel left out
left behind
marginalized

not included, lost
trying to re-enter, re-define, re-phrase
searching for spirituality and community
searching for a multicultural, multiracial community
searching for a community accepting of all
        sexual orientations
searching for a community of festival and celebration
many strong individuals
with many different agendas, talents and gifts
all searching for you
and for their spiritual center
beautiful people, seekers
of accepting community
loving welcome
and celebrating worship
but often not knowing where to look
or for what or for whom to look.
Loving God,
continue to be pleased with
and bless the ministry I do
and the spiritual journey I am on.
  I am grateful for the appearance
  of your messenger of heavenly
  reassurance and joy.
God, see me through, forever
forgive me, compassionately
empower me, always
bless my life, eternally
overcome my weaknesses and failures, affirmingly
renew my creativity, constantly
nurture my openness, endlessly
heal my body, mind and spirit, daily

restore my freedom, continuously
refresh my joy, ceaselessly
give me direction, faith, and hope
health, love, and peace
a calming of my inner restlessness
until the end of my time.
   May The Lord Of The Dance
   never leave me
   may The Hound Of Heaven
   never stop pursuing me.
May celebration always define me
may the Zorbic always embrace my spirit
may my simple roots
   and humble abilities
   be adequate
   for the journey
   of my time.
May my simple roots
and humble abilities
be adequate
for the journey
of this time
of this day.

A Sunday Morning Personal Prayer

This prayer was inspired by words in Habakkuk Chapter Three. It is brief and to the point. It was a prayer prayed for twenty years in the yearning and restlessness of my own heart every Sunday morning before the people arrived. It is a prayer for transformational leaders. The succinct prayer attempts to keep God, personal spirituality, and ministerial calling in perspective. I would literally never dare to begin Sunday morning without it.

God,
I have heard and read
    of what you have done
and I am filled with awe.
Now do again in this time
    in this place
    (today, this year)
    the great deeds
    you used to do.
And God, be merciful
be merciful
use even ME
use EVEN me
as an instrument
a messenger
a cheerleader
an apostle
of your loving grace
and your gracious love.
Amen.

A Psalm

Sometimes a popular psalm, hymn, song, biblical verse, or prayer can become so familiar that it loses its spiritual edge. For me, that was never the case with Psalm Twenty-three. I always read different versions, and even frequently created my own. This psalm is a great transformational leader's constant companion along an ever-evolving faith and an ever-changing life-journey terrain. The Twenty-third Psalm works best as a companion if it is read and repeated often, until it becomes a part of the very essence of one's being.

God is my shepherd
I shall not want
God makes me lie down
In green pastures
Leads me beside still waters
Restores my soul
Leads me in right paths
For God's name's sake
Even though I walk
Through the valley of
Shadows and uncertainty
I fear no evil
For you are with me
Your rod and your staff —
They comfort me
You prepare a table before me
In the presence of my enemies
You anoint my head with oil
My cup overflows
Surely goodness and mercy
Shall follow me
All the days of my life
And I shall dwell
In the house of God
My whole life long!

A Song

There are many songs, hymns, spirituals, and anthems that contribute to a transformational leader's well-examined life. I share this one because it was in my mind and heart every day and because, even though it is familiar and easily sung, it took me years before I could sing all the words. I needed to first get rid of some of my own baggage and some of the song's baggage before I could let the song enter deep into my being. To sing "Amazing Grace" is to travel miles, years, and decades down an emotional, personal, spiritual, moral, and social journey.

Amazing grace, how sweet the sound,
That saved a wretch like me!
I once was lost, but now am found,
Was blind but now I see.
   Through many dangers, toils, and snares,
   I have already come;
   'Tis grace has brought me safe thus far,
   And grace will lead me home.
My God has promised good to me,
Whose word my hope secures;
God will my shield and portion be
As long as life endures.

Epilogue

Succession
Giving the essential spirit of Middle a chance to thrive

A new thing was definitely created in the earth at Second Avenue and 7th Street. There wasn't anything quite like it in New York City. For the sake of this wonderfully new, unconventional, and diverse congregation, I did not want either me or Middle to ever become static, stuck on a plateau, relying on past successes, losing our bit of relevant edginess, and feeling satisfied with where we were and what we had accomplished.

A prayer that was constantly in my mind is that God would give me the insight to know and the courage to accept the timing of my time at Middle. It is too prevalent among clergy that we are unable to know and incapable of accepting the timing of our time in the ministry. We clergy somehow feel we still have it; we still have the fire inside us, we still are capable of being on the cutting edge long after the timing of our time has come and gone. Few friends, colleagues, denominational executives, boards, and church members are willing to be truthful with us. As we age it is easy for us to become satisfied with the status quo and blind to what is actually happening right in front of us with staff, ministry, congregation, neighborhood, and city. I did not want this to happen to me or to Middle Church. Every Saturday morning, sitting behind Middle's old stone pulpit in the silence of an empty sanctuary, I prayed, "God, give me the insight to know and the courage to accept the timing of my time at Middle."

The insight was churning in my soul. The "still small voice" became clearer and clearer. I now needed to have courage. Finally, in June 2002, I confided in the board. Their response was, "But you look, think, and act so much younger than you are." "The whole congregation came here because of your ministry." "There will be people in the congregation who won't come back, if you leave." "You still have it." "We are still a creative and growing congregation." "Middle is a very special, in some respects, unique place—where will we ever find someone to replace you?" Then they tried to compromise, saying, "We will do more of the work and also get more volunteers to help." "Do we need more staff to lighten up your too busy schedule?" "We love you too much and you are too important to this church for you to leave right now." This, of course, is exactly what we clergy love to hear. Our egos are boosted, our persons are charged, and we feel guilty for even suggesting the possibility of moving on. The fact is, I did still have a large reservoir of energy and ideas. I still was creative and loved people and ministry. Secretly, I had always believed I was ahead of my time, so I could coast at this ministry thing for a while and still be relevant. But other senior ministers in the history of Middle Church may have thought that, too, while right before them the church was static or declining, the neighborhood and city were changing, the daily challenges were getting harder, the once patient personality was getting crankier, and the ministry and vision remained the same for too long.

I promised that would never again happen at Middle. I was determined that history was not going to repeat itself on my watch. The insight was clear. I led Middle Church from near death to a growing, creative, thriving, arts friendly, diverse, multicultural, multiracial, multi-sexual orientation, festive ministry with a significant outreach to the neighborhood, city, and region. Middle now needed fresh leadership with new skills and dreams. Someone who would be committed to the essential spirit of Middle, while creating a new vision for the next exciting phase of Middle's life, ministry, worship, outreach, education, and growth.

The members of Middle's board were lovingly supportive and incredibly courageous. Because of the church's special ministry style and spirit, it was decided to follow a succession process, rather than a traditional search and interim minister procedure. The most important first step was for the board to compile a list of items that was called "The Essential Middle." The board intended for the essential spirit of Middle to continue beyond my retirement, even though the new senior minister would be encouraged to develop and implement a new vision and strategic plan to lead Middle Church into its next new and exciting phase of life, ministry, and growth.

Since the new person would be a Collegiate senior minister in charge of Middle Collegiate Church, the succession committee consisted of members of Middle's board as well as the boards of Marble, West End, and Fort Washington Collegiate churches. From its beginning in 1628, the Collegiate Church of New York City had only white male senior ministers. Diverse, multi-gender, multiracial, multicultural leaders at the highest senior levels of a church's leadership are still uncommon because it does not just automatically happen, especially in significant or larger churches. More of the same is what naturally happens. For such diversity to take place at the senior level of leadership of a major church, it must be purposeful. Some one, some group, some committee, some board has to step up and intentionally offer a positive pathway to change, otherwise it won't happen. Everybody knows that, but often the courage or the political will or the transformational leadership is lacking. The traditional search process in a church is always advertised as "open," but it rarely produces anything other than what it has always produced.

Portraits of senior ministers hang in the four Collegiate Churches. They are all male, all white. It was my very transparent choice to advocate for the next portrait to be hung at Middle Collegiate Church to be of a woman senior minister. It was intentional that the succession process sought out some of the best women leaders in the country, although it was obviously receptive to all applicants. During the search there were conversations with several men, but in the end it was two women who rose to the top of the committee's consideration. To help narrow it to a single selection, the two candidates were interviewed together by the same psychologist who interviewed me twenty years earlier and by a meeting of the senior ministers of the other Collegiate churches and the senior staff of the Collegiate Church Corporation and Board.

On May 4, 2003, Jacqui Lewis was unanimously recommended to become the Associate Collegiate Minister at Middle Collegiate Church with the intention of succeeding me as the senior minister when I retired. Jacqui and I worked together for eighteen months in one of the most enjoyable, creative, and collegial partnerships in all my forty years in the ministry. On September 12, 2004, I announced to the congregation my intention to retire effective at the end of June, 2005. Following the worship celebration I led an informal conversation with the congregation. On January 23, 2005, I announced that Jacqui would succeed me when I retired. There was a standing ovation for Jacqui following the announcement. After the worship celebration, both Jacqui and I led a second informal conversation with the congregation. On June 30, 2005, I retired and my dear friend and one of the most gifted and capable persons I know succeeded me as the senior minister of Middle Collegiate Church. She is the one who can boldly lead Middle in a new vision beyond where I could possibly go. Middle's yo-yo history will not repeat itself. And the next senior minister portrait hanging on the wall of Middle Church will be of an African-American woman. The church's wall of history will be changed forever.

Selected Bibliography

Adams, Douglas, *The Prostitute in the Family Tree: Discovering Humor and Irony in the Bible,* Westminster John Knox Press, 1997.

Adams, Douglas, *Humor in the American Pulpit from George Whitefield through Henry Ward Beecher,* The Sharing Company, 1976.

Adams, Douglas, and Apostolos-Cappadona, Diane, Editors, *Dance as Religious Studies,* The Crossroad Publishing Company, 1990.

Barna, George, *Turn-Around Churches: How to Overcome Barriers to Growth and Bring New Life to an Established Church,* Regal Books, 1993.

Chesnut, Robert A., *Transforming the Mainline Church,* Geneva Press, 2000.

Ehrman, Bart D., *Misquoting Jesus: The Story Behind Who Changed the Bible and Why,* HarperSanFrancisco, 2005.

Garten, Jeffrey E., *The Mind of the C.E.O.,* Basic Books, New York, 1995.

Glasse, James D., *Putting It Together in the Parish,* Abingdon Press, 1972.

Granberg-Michaelson, Wesley, *Leadership From Inside Out: Spirituality and Organizational Change,* The Crossroads Publishing Company, 2006.

Heifetz, Ronald A., *Leadership Without Easy Answers,* Harvard University Press, 1994.

Heifetz, Ronald A. and Marty Linsky, *Leadership on the Line: Staying Alive through the Dangers of Leading,* Harvard Business School Publishing, 2002.

Herrington, Jim, *Leading Congregational Change: A Practical Guide for the Transformational Journey,* Jossey-Bass Publishers, 2000.

Huber, Jane Parker, *A Singing Faith,* Westminster John Knox Press, 1987.

Hyers, Conrad, *The Comic Vision and the Christian Faith: A Celebration of Life and Laughter,* The Pilgrim Press, 1981.

Kotter, John P., *Leading Change,* Harvard Business School Press, 1996.

Long, Thomas G., *Beyond the Worship Wars: Building Vital and Faithful Worship,* The Alban Institute, 2001.

Maitland, Sara, *A Big Enough God: A Feminist's Search for a Joyful Theology,* H. Holt, 1995.

Maitland, Sara, *A Joyful Theology: Creation, Commitment, and an Awesome God,* Augsburg Books, 2002.

Payne, Robert, *The Great God Plan,* Hermitage House, New York, 1952.

Rock, Judith and Norman Mealy, *Performer as Priest & Prophet,* Harper & Row Publishers, 1988.

The New Century Hymnal, The Pilgrim Press, 1995.

The New Testament and Psalms: An Inclusive Version, Oxford University Press, 1995; an adaptation using the *New Revised Standard Version Bible,* National Council of the Churches of Christ in the U.S.A., 1989.

The Inclusive Hebrew Scriptures, Volume I: The Torah, Priests for Equality, 2000.

The Inclusive Hebrew Scriptures, Volume III: The Writings, Priests for Equality, 1999.

Weems, Lovett H., *Church Leadership: Vision, Team Culture, and Integrity,* Abingdon Press, 1993.

Weems, Lovett H., *Take the Next Step: Leading Lasting Change in the Church,* Abingdon Press, 2003.

Wise, Tim, *White Like Me: Reflections on Race from a Privileged Son,* Soft Skull Press, 2005.

Acknowledgements

Writing this book has made me very aware of how much I am indebted to so many people, places, and experiences. The book would never have been written without the inspiration, suggestions, and guidance of Mark Shaw, my consultant and mentor throughout the entire project. The thirty-year friendship and encouragement of Doug Adams is woven through the book's entire footprint. I am grateful Doug was able to write the foreword prior to his untimely death. The helpful comments of the readers—Doug Adams, Gayle Dragt, Jacqui Lewis, Hak Joon Lee, and Mark Shaw—made the book more complete than I could have ever done by myself. With professional skill and personal humor, editor Nancy Crenshaw shaped my words into a "real" manuscript. Early in the writing process Ana Cerro assisted with editorial suggestions. Stella Jackson, Director of Editing Services, American Book Publishing (ABP), carefully chose the perfect editor for the manuscript and me. A special thanks to ABP editor, Lindsey Winsemius, who refreshingly viewed her task as an active partnership between editor and author. Lindsey's helpful comments and suggestions were always accompanied by welcomed encouragement and sprinkled with subtle humor and more understanding than I could have ever imagined. My wife, Gayle, was an important partner, encouraging, reading all the drafts, providing relationship space to make it possible for me to write, and for so many years modeling intentional leadership by continuously challenging the traditional role of a minister's spouse. Thanks to the leaders and members of Second Reformed Church, Pebble Hill Church, Tappan Reformed Church, and The Community Church of Chapel Hill for nurturing me along the way and influencing my passion for intentional leadership. Thanks to the Collegiate Church Corporation for calling me to Middle and supporting and celebrating the entire journey to rescue Middle from near death. Of course, the book would not be possible without the special Collegiate and Middle boards, ministers, staff, long-time Middle administrator, Nora Fragosa, and congregation of Middle Collegiate Church. For twenty years we traveled an incredibly adventurous journey together, resurrecting an unconventional new church out of old and tired bones. That extraordinary transformational journey and how it can inspire, encourage and challenge other church leaders and congregations is the subject of this book.

About the Author

Gordon Dragt has an AB from Hope College, BD from Western Theological Seminary, and ThM from Princeton Theological Seminary. He is a member of the adjunct faculty of The Center for the Arts, Religion, and Education in the field of worship and the arts, sponsored by the Graduate Theological Union in Berkeley, CA.; a Fellow in the Society for Arts, Religion, and Contemporary Culture; was honored as Arts Minister of the Year by The Center for the Arts, Religion, and Education; has thirty-five years of experience transforming declining town, suburban, and city churches into thriving arts-friendly, multicultural and multiracial congregations; and has numerous other awards, honors, and certifications. Gordon has served on the Board of Trustees of New Brunswick Theological Seminary in New Brunswick,

NJ, and is currently on the seminary's Anti-Racism Team and Artist in Residence Committee. Gordon is Emeritus Senior Minister of the Collegiate Churches of NYC, where he served for twenty years as Senior Minister of Middle Collegiate Church, during which time it was transformed from a dying church into a dynamic and diverse city-wide ministry to over one thousand people.